The Undiminished Man

By Janet Stevenson

Books

Novels: *Weep No More* (Viking Press)
           The Ardent Years (Viking Press)
           Sisters and Brothers (Crown)

Travel: *Woman Aboard* (Crown)

Biographies for Young Readers

Spokesman for Freedom: Archibald Grimké
   (Crowell Collier)
John James Audubon: Painting America's Wild Life
   (Encyclopedia Britannica Books)
Marian Anderson: Singing to the World
   (Encyclopedia Britannica Books)
Pioneers in Freedom (Reilly & Lee)
Soldiers in the Civil Rights War (Reilly & Lee)
First Book of Women's Rights (Franklin Watts)
The Montgomery Bus Boycott (Franklin Watts)
Brown v. Board of Education (Franklin Watts)

Articles (including one on Robert Walker Kenny) in *American Heritage*, 1963 to 1979; also, articles for *Atlantic Monthly* and other periodicals.

The Undiminished Man

A political biography of Robert Walker Kenny

Janet Stevenson

Chandler & Sharp Publishers, Inc.
Novato, California

Photograph Sources and Credits: Frontispiece, by Cleo Trumbo and Pauline Finn; page 28, by Jack Berman; page 39, courtesy California Archives; page 57, courtesy *The Dispatcher* (ILWU); page 97, courtesy Corinth Films; pages 115 and 135, courtesy Meiklejohn Civil Liberties Institute, Berkeley, California. The photographs on pages 8, 64, 67 (photograph by Walter R. Scheibel), 132, 154, and the front jacket (photograph by Walter R. Scheibel) are from the files of Robert Walker Kenny; back-jacket photograph, courtesy *Peoples World*; the jacket photograph of Janet Stevenson is by Wyn Berry.

Library of Congress Cataloging in Publication Data

Stevenson, Janet.
  The undiminished man.

  Includes index.
  1. Kenny, Robert Walker, 1901–1976. 2. California
—Politics and government—1846–1950. 3. Law—
California—History and criticism. 4. Legislators—
California—Biography. 5. California. Legislature.
Senate—Biography. 6. Judges—California—Biography.
I. Title.
F866.K35S75   979.4'05'0924 [B]   80–10889
ISBN 0-88316-538–4

Copyright © 1980 by Janet Stevenson.
All rights reserved.
International Standard Book Number: 0-88316-538–4
Library of Congress Catalog Card Number: 80–10889
Printed in the United States of America.

Book and jacket design by Kerry Tremain.
Editor: Peter N. Carroll.
Composition by Marin Typesetters.

To Robert Morris, without whom neither Robert Kenny's contribution nor this account of it would have been possible.

CONTENTS

FOREWORD

NATIONALLY KNOWN AND ADMIRED, BOB KENNY OCcupied a special niche in the affections of Californians—Left, Right, or Center—for reasons which outsiders never fully accepted or understood. Light-hearted, witty, whimsical—a merry-andrew type—he had an immense relish for the ease and comfort of good living. His mother once said that before he died he would probably be on a first-name basis with the headwaiter of every good restaurant in the state, and he came close to achieving that distinction. He liked people, all kinds of people, and he wanted them to like him, as most of those who knew him did. He was regarded with admiration and affection by an incredibly large and astonishingly mixed assortment of Californians: cabdrivers, bartenders, educators, scientists, bankers, industrialists, intellectuals, lobbyists, lawyers, socialites, doctors, jurists, politicians, truckdrivers, farm workers, growers, wine merchants, bail-bond brokers, roustabouts, longshoremen, actors and actresses, screenwriters and directors, ministers, priests and rabbis, men and women, blacks, Chicanos, Orientals, rich and poor and middle class.

His wisecracks and sallies, never in short supply, were quoted from one end of the state to the other. He was a politician's politician and the delight of reporters and editors. For years his office was the first port of call for visiting political bigwigs and journalists who wanted to be briefed on the state's volatile politics.

When he was president of the National Lawyers Guild in the 1940s, defending "reds" and "radicals," he looked forward with pleasure to attending the regular monthly meetings of the board of directors of the Citizens National Bank of which he was a member. The other directors, one may be sure, enjoyed his company if they did not always accept his advice. An easy touch, he had a lively sympathy for underdogs and down-and-outers. He detested hypocrites, the excessively self-righteous, and humbugs of all varieties.

The late Chief Justice of the U.S. Supreme Court, Earl Warren, and Bob Kenny were good friends, and in a subtle way, tacit collaborators. Kenny had been responsible in no small

Robert Walker Kenny

measure for Warren's election as attorney general in 1938. At some considerable political risk he endorsed Warren, who had cross-filed in the Democratic primary; the endorsement, not appreciated by Kenny's fellow Democrats, was a significant factor in Warren's election.   Before issuing the endorsement, Kenny obtained a handwritten letter in which Warren stated that he shared his friend's commitment to civil liberties. The letter was widely circulated in the campaign and was extremely good politics for Warren, who, up to that time and in fact until his appointment to the Supreme Court, had a bleak-to-dismal record on civil liberties and civil rights. But it is a measure of Kenny's sagacity that once Warren got where he wanted to be—the Supreme Court—he honored his earlier commitment to civil liberties.

In 1942, when Warren decided to run for Governor, he let it be known that if Kenny ran for attorney general, the Republicans would not be displeased. That is, Warren endorsed Kenny by implication. Kenny was the only Democrat to win election to a statewide office that year. As a wartime attorney general, he was wholly admirable. Warren had forcefully advocated the mass evacuation of all Japanese Americans and later took the position that none should be permitted to return to California until the end of the war. But Kenny managed to win his cooperation and support, along with that of the local law-enforcement officials—no small chore in itself—and so the returning evacuees encountered only minor acts of hostility. He was also largely responsible for the prompt restoration of civic order at the time of the "zoot-suit" race riots in Los Angeles.

In 1946 he was dragooned into running against Warren, largely because he was the strongest candidate the belatedly formed New Deal Democratic Party in California could come up with. No one knew better than canny Bob Kenny that his chances against Warren were miniscule, but he was under great pressure from liberal Democrats and left-wing elements to make the race. The entire Democratic slate, including Edmund G. Brown, running for attorney general, and Will Rogers, Jr., the party's nominee for U.S. Senate, went down to defeat.

That election wrote finis to Kenny's political career. The cold war had begun in 1945 and as it heated up he was increasingly motivated to oppose it, appearing as counsel for the Hollywood Ten and defending many others whose civil liberties were under attack. From 1940 to 1949 he was president of the National Lawyers Guild (he was one of the founders); few lawyers of his prominence would have welcomed the assignment in those years, but he accepted the burdens—and the often vicious redbaiting—with his usual good nature, never taking himself too seriously, never losing his cool.

At the time of his retirement the Los Angeles Bar Association voted to give him the Shattuck-Price Award for distinguished service to the legal profession, in part no doubt by way of making amends for past slights and oversights. On this occasion Kenny was asked what he had done in the course of his career of which he was most proud. It was, he replied, the eight years in the late 1940s and 1950s during which he had spent most of his time defending so-called "reds" and "radicals" who had been denied their constitutional rights. One may be sure that Bob Kenny did not sacrifice his political career lightly; politics was his life's blood. He did what he thought he had to do. He will be long remembered in California. Nor will Californians ever see his like again, not ever.

Janet Stevenson's biography provides an invaluable source to the on-coming generation about Robert Kenny's extraordinarily interesting career and the unique role he played in California politics. And his friends, who are legion, will treasure it. In California there is always an acute need to understand the politics of recent years since the cultural scene changes so rapidly before it has been fully chronicled. This memoir illuminates events and relationships that are already in danger of being eclipsed by the ruthless process of rapid social change in a state which is never today what it was the day before yesterday.

Carey McWilliams

PREFACE

ONE OF THE ACCOMPLISHMENTS OF THE DOmestic witchhunt conducted during the presidency of Harry S. Truman by committees of the House of Representatives and Senate (and their imitators on state and local levels) was to expunge from the national memory what the late Senator Joseph McCarthy of Wisconsin liked to refer to as "twenty years of treason" and others called the New Deal.

Roosevelt's image has survived, but that's about all. There is hardly a mention of most of the supporting players or the struggles, victories, and defeats of that dramatic and momentous period in the textbooks used by most students of U.S. history, hardly a trace of their existence in the consciousness of the new generation of citizens.

This strange hiatus in the record has recently begun to concern historians. Oral history projects have been established in universities, and young scholars are seeking out men and women who played significant roles in the Roosevelt era, recording their reminiscences while they are still "available for comment."

It is out of one such oral history project that this book was born.

In the early 1960s, Doyce Nunis of the University of California spent several days taping Robert Walker Kenny's account of his "first forty years in California politics." Kenny was at that time retired from active political life, after a career that roughly mirrored the rise and fall of the New Deal.

When a transcript of the interview was sent to him, Kenny was dismayed at the inaccuracy of his off-the-cuff narration and, being at the time only partially occupied by a desultory law practice, he took the time to go over his notes, letters, clippings, and official papers, and to dictate from them a revised version. This was mimeographed and circulated among some 200 friends and acquaintances whose comments he solicited.

The consensus was that while the manuscript contained valuable historical material, it had serious shortcomings. The one most often mentioned was that Kenny's own character and personality, his remarkable abilities and equally remarkable failings, were missing. The Kenny wit, which had operated as the ack-ack of resistance to HUAC repression, was killed in his retelling of his best wisecracks. His analysis of issues and personalities, always acute and sometimes profound, was blunted by his reluctance to say unkind things, however true, in cold, enduring print. And there was no perspective on his own performance in the arena of history.

Several people suggested that the memoirs be reworked with a collaborator. But before Kenny could be persuaded to invest more time in the effort, his situation changed. When the oral historians first approached him, he had been "unemployed and bored into garrulousness." But in the last hours of Governor Edmund (Pat) Brown's last term of office, he appointed Kenny to the Superior Court of Los Angeles County. Back in the harness he had worn at the start of his public life, Kenny had no energy to spare for the remembrance of things past.

He asked me to do the reworking without him.

"I don't really want a collaborator," he wrote. "I want you to write something in the third person, so that I can be included in the gallery of Abolitionists and oddballs to whom your biographical talents have been devoted. I like to think of you at a typewriter batting out the Kenny fable while I can go out and cheer for the Giants."

I agreed to this division of labor mainly because I had—and still have—a sense of deep indebtedness to Bob Kenny. Much (though not all) of it stems from the time he functioned as my "non-attorney," or to put it his way, when I functioned as his "guided missile."

In November 1956, I was served with a subpoena directing me to appear at a hearing of the House UnAmerican Activities Committee to be held in Los Angeles on December 7—the fifteenth Anniversary of Pearl Harbor!

This was, as it turned out, the last foray of the HUAC hunters into the Hollywood game preserve. They were scraping the bottom of the barrel for witnesses, having long since run through the roster of citizens connected with the entertainment industry, including the lawyers, doctors, dentists, and optometrists who took care of them.

The political profit to be derived from the staging of yet another public inquisition had dropped so low that cynics were suggesting that the congressmen were just getting in their last free junket to the beaches of Santa Monica. But the consequences of a confrontation with them were still economically serious.

The blacklist was unbroken except in the field of television and film writing. Even there, the structure of the black market was so delicate that the slightest ripple of publicity produced panic. Also, to complicate matters for my "class" of victims, there was consensus among us that the time had come for counterattack. New positions vis-à-vis the committee were being worked out by lawyers and debated by witnesses-to-be, the objective being to strike the most powerful blow possible at the committee's questionable constitutionality without going to jail for one's pains.

Against this background, I put my pink slip in my pocket, went to call on my neighbor and friend, Robert Kenny, and asked if he would take me as a client.

Kenny said no.

I knew he had become increasingly reluctant to appear as counsel to witnesses at HUAC hearings as the behavior of committee members and their counsels increasingly departed from established rules of jurisprudence and standards of fair play. "Having a lawyer up there with a witness makes it look as if the lawyer could do something he can't do," Kenny said. "We're contributing to the misleading impression that this is a court. Acting as a sort of legal fig leaf."

But he had continued to accompany clients to the pillory until the U.S. Supreme Court decision in the Watkins case. This, he explained to me, "established that the committee itself must advise the witness of his rights and privileges under the Constitution.

"No one really needs a lawyer any more. All you need is to be able to hold up five fingers or five toes." More soberly he went on to explain that "they're not supposed to ask you entrapping questions or questions that aren't related to some legislative purpose. In other words: 'No fishing!'

"That's all you have to remember to remind them. But if you think you need a warm-up before you go to bat, I could stop over some afternoon and put you through a rehearsal."

I accepted the proposal of going it alone. But as one after the other of my fourteen days of waiting passed without a word from my "non-attorney," I could feel my anxiety level rising. Finally, Bob showed up on Saturday morning, December 3, looking unusually shabby in a rumpled sports shirt, a much-mended cardigan, and a pair of pants that could have passed for pajama bottoms.

For less than an hour, interrupted by questions from my sons about baseball statistics (all of which Bob answered accurately), he played the devil's advocate (or committee counsel) while I practiced using the two "ploys" he had brought along, typed on blue file cards.

Ploy Number One read: "I object to the question on the

ground that it does not pertain to any legislative purpose, and I request a formal ruling from the chairman on that point." Or, "What is the legislative purpose of your question?"

Ploy Number Two was subtitled the Specific Ploy: "If you have any specific matter you want to question me about in relation to my motion pictures (or family, or anything else they might be getting into), I wish you would direct my attention to it." This was supposed to prevent the committee's counsel from wandering over the open range of my political past and present.

There was also a third ploy, not on a card, which appealed to the committee's responsibility to protect my constitutional rights from invasion by its own questions.

Bob began firing questions that dealt with what was rumored to be the "target area" of this particular hearing: the Los Angeles Committee for Protection of the Foreign Born and its anti-McCarran Act campaign. For example: "Is it true that in March of last year you chaired a so-called workshop on ways to evade the consequences of violating the law of our land in the matter of . . . etc., etc.?"

Every now and then Bob would deliver a change-up that explored a totally unrelated activity, such as, "Isn't it true that you were a member of the Screen Writers' Guild while it was under the domination of the international Communist conspiracy?"

Little by little, I learned how to play my ploy cards: Ploy One when the question was clearly unrelated to any legislative proposal under consideration by Congress (since investigation with an eye to law-making was the committee's legal raison d'être). Ploy Two, when I couldn't see just where the questions were leading. Ploy Three, the appeal to the chairman, when I could see the trap.

On the morning of my appearance, Bob called to wish me luck and to say he would be at home and available by phone. He expected a play-by-play account as soon as I was off the stand. He was "sort of sorry" it wasn't going to be carried on radio or TV because he was sure I was going to wait for a "gopher" ball and hit it out of the park. Or, if the committee was smarter than he expected it to be, draw an intentional base on balls.

I marched to the witness stand that morning feeling more like Joan of Arc than a home-run hitter, fingering the small blue cards with which I was going to try to smother the committee's fire. It seemed a frail hope, but it was too late to call for an auxiliary engine.

Ploy Number One got a laugh the first time I used it. Chairman Clyde Doyle's gavel banged and the audience quieted. Committee Counsel Richard Arens, who was doing a creditable imitation of Joe McCarthy, began a long, involved question that started with my teaching in the drama department of the University of Southern California and ended with the "international Communist conspiracy." I probably should have used Ploy Two, but I had forgotten the wording and didn't want to look. So I resorted to Ploy Three and asked the chairman whether it was advisable for me to answer.

Congressman Doyle said that he was not my lawyer and if I wanted legal advice he was willing to excuse me until the following day so I could go out and retain one. I said I didn't need a lawyer. The committee had to protect me from entrapment. The Watkins decision said so.

This got an even louder laugh from the audience. More gavelling. A quick, inaudible conference between the committee members present. Then a last entrapping question: "Are you a Communist?" (For some reason, the traditional "or have you ever been" was omitted.)

I stood on "all my constitutional rights—all the amendments" and was abruptly dismissed.

My gratitude to Bob Kenny was not so much for having protected me from entrapment and its consequences, as for having shown me the way to land what I felt was a blow at the solar plexus of the archenemy. It is true that subsequent changes in the wording of HUAC counsels' questions cut some of the ground from the beachhead I had helped establish. But by that time HUAC was on its way to dissolution anyway.

The book that has resulted from my "non-collaboration" with Kenny has turned out to be something more than a reworking of his manuscript. Fleshing out his account of events involved many taped interviews, some with him, some with colleagues in every stage of his career, from his days as a lobbyist in Sacramento where he first worked with Earl Warren, to his last years on the bench when he stirred the John Birchers into a recall campaign.

In our later conversations Kenny was less interested in answering questions about details of his political life than in placing it in perspective. He was reading revisionist historians of the Cold War like D.H. Fleming and Gar Alperovitz and urged me to do the same. Perhaps he hoped I would be inspired to attempt a real contribution to the growing body of scholarship they represent.

My own hopes are more modest. What I have tried to write is a political—not a scholarly—biography, addressed to the men and women who, without knowing it, are Bob Kenny's spiritual and political heirs.

There was a time when the leaders of the New Left advised their followers to waste no time reading history but to get on with the doing of their own thing. I believe the two courses are not mutually exclusive, and that there is some reason to assume that "he who does not know history is doomed to repeat it."

Funds for the travel necessary to interview key figures in Kenny's story were provided by a grant from the Rabinowitz Foundation. I had access to the Kenny papers in the Bancroft Library of the University of California, and the generous cooperation of hundreds of Kenny's colleagues. Very few of those who worked with or for him over the years were reluctant to talk about their experiences. Ex-Governor Pat Brown was the only one who failed to respond to a request for an interview.

But by far the greatest contribution to my effort was made by Robert Morris, Kenny's longtime friend and law partner. The friendship between the two Bobs was deeper and more durable than many blood relationships. In many ways Bob Morris acted the part of the son Bob Kenny never had.

It was Bob Morris who supplied details missing in the original manuscript and corrected small inaccuracies I could not have caught without help. He produced papers Kenny had forgotten he had and supplied insights that no one else could. Above all, he demanded that I finish the job when Kenny's interest in it evaporated and my energies flagged.

"I consider myself incredibly lucky to have spent most of my professional life in daily contact with a man like Kenny," he said once. "It just about kills me that no one recognizes his stature—his contribution. There's nothing I wouldn't do to make sure it gets on paper and between covers while I'm around to enjoy it."

Bob Morris died suddenly in 1977, less than a year after Bob Kenny's death. He had seen a rough draft of the book, and he was happy with it. I believe he would accept the dedication of the final version as a symbol of his dedication to its subject even though his extreme, but genuine modesty would have prevented his accepting my assessment of his own role in Kenny's career.

Janet Stevenson

The Undiminished Man

1.

Amicus Curiae

THE ATMOSPHERE IN THE CHAMBER OF THE U.S. Supreme Court is awe-inspiring. The nine black-robed justices sit like a row of graven images. On those rare occasions when one of them is moved to speak, the accoustics so distort his voice that it seems to come from a great distance. As a lawyer approaches the lectern on which he is permitted to rest his papers while making oral argument, one almost expects him to genuflect. It is a rare person who is not intimidated.

On this particular morning there had not been a single question or comment by any of the nine. The first of three attorneys for the defense in *Yates et al.* v. *the U.S.* had been heard in silence. A sense of prejudgement—negative—was heavy in the air.

The second of the defense lawyers came to the lectern: a short, plump, middle-aged man, soberly and conventionally dressed except for a prefabricated bow-tie nestling coyly under his jowls, walking with the reluctant shamble of one who would have preferred to take a cab, keeping his right hand thrust into his pocket to conceal a malformed and useless arm.

As the newcomer settled his thin sheaf of papers and pulled his glasses lower on his nose, the man in the center of the long black line leaned forward. "Good morning, Judge Kenny," said Chief Justice Earl Warren.

A susurrus of surprise ran along the rows of spectators. Reporters asked each other who Kenny was and why the Chief should single him out for this unusual courtesy. What made it all the more surprising was that Yates et al. were a bunch of Communists, the latest to appeal their conviction under the Smith Act. All of their predecessors before the court had gone to jail for advocating the overthrow of the United States or something in that line.   There was no reason to think these defendants were going to get off any easier.

But Kenny was making jokes instead of an argument! He explained that he appeared on behalf of only one defendant, William Schneiderman, whom he had represented twenty years earlier in a denaturalization suit.   The charge then was that Schneiderman had falsely sworn allegiance when he became a citizen since his avowed membership in the Communist Party was proof that he intended to overthrow the government.

The case had been lost in the lower court but won on appeal before the Supreme Court where it had been argued by Wendell Willkie.   The point Kenny was making, almost facetiously, was that the decision in the first case constituted proof of Schneiderman's innocence in this one.

"It's like the fellow who has done time in a mental institution and been discharged as cured.   He's got a certificate that says he's sane.   Any time anybody wants to challenge that, he can pull it out and say 'I've got a paper that says I'm not crazy. Where's yours?' " (RWK)*

Several of the stone faces cracked into smiles. Suddenly the majesty of the court seemed less inhuman. Communication was possible because the man at the lectern was speaking to his peers.

All this would have been less astonishing to an audience of Kenny's fellow Californians. They knew him as a man who commanded respect from all bands of the political spectrum, ranging from right-wing political hacks who rose to high office, to the beleaguered representatives of the proletariat he was defending here.

They knew him also as the youngest man ever appointed to a judgeship in his home state;

as the state senator who in a single term blazed legislative trails it took twenty years fully to clear;

as the only Democrat to hold state office in the Republican regime of Governor Earl Warren—which made Kenny the leading California Democrat in the years of President Roosevelt's incumbency;

as the man who might very well have been Vice-President of the United States when Roosevelt died;

* THROUGHOUT THIS BOOK the designation (RWK) will be used when the person quoted is Robert W. Kenny.

as a man who had never lost an election until he ran against Warren for the governorship and never won an election after that;

as the man whose influence on Warren was the main source of the change in the Chief Justice's political philosophy that baffled the President who appointed him.

Viewed from the perspective of another twenty years, Robert Walker Kenny is even more impressive than he looked that day in the Supreme Court—more than the sum of all his distinctions.

He is the quintessential New Deal man—an almost perfect example of the citizen-politician that produced and was produced by the left-center coalition that came to power in the United States in the early years of Franklin D. Roosevelt's presidency.

Kenny's story is the story of that coalition: how it was formed; what it was at its best; what it could have been; and what happened to it when Roosevelt was succeeded by the man Kenny called "an ignorant, malevolent border politician."

It is a story worth telling for its own sake and for its relevance to the future of our ailing republic.

2.
The Myth of Invincibility

I N A LITTLE LESS THAN TWENTY YEARS ROBERT Walker Kenny rose from the lowest rung on the state's political ladder to the rung nearest to the top. Yet he never had the backing of any real party organization or a real campaign chest. Nor did he ever hesitate to take and hold a controversial position in which he believed.

The combination of boldness and nonchalance that became known as the Kenny style was rooted in a soil well composted with indifference. Kenny never really gave much of a damn whether he won or lost a campaign for office. He was never sure he should have gotten into politics in the first place. "All I ever really wanted to be," he said once in his later years, "was a newspaperman."

Kenny was an undergraduate at Stanford University in 1920 when he got his start in journalism. Having been freed from the time-consuming pursuit of athletic honors by a birth injury that crippled his right arm, he loafed through the required course of study and concentrated on his extracurricular duties as a reporter for the *Daily Palo Altoan* and campus correspondent for the United Press. One of the important news stories of that day was the unsolved mystery of whether Herbert Hoover, who had just returned to his home on the Stanford campus after completing his highly publicized job with Belgian Relief, was a Republican or a Democrat.

"Despite the fact that there were special correspondents for national newspapers all over the city of Palo Alto, Mr. Hoover decided to release his fateful selection, when he made it, through the campus wire services, which meant that Landis Weaver of the A.P. and Robert Kenny of the U.P. scooped the rest of the Fourth Estate." (RWK)

From this auspicious beginning, Kenny graduated to a brief tenure as financial editor of the *Los Angeles Times.* (The newspaper's owner, Harry Chandler, "had been a friend of my late father, and he felt he ought to do something for Bob Kenny's boy, Bob.") (RWK) In 1922, Bob married and took his bride, the former Sara McCann, to London where he served as representative of the United Press and to Paris where he worked on the *Tribune.* The Kennys came back to Los Angeles in 1923, and Bob landed a job as court reporter for the Hearst morning paper, the *Express.*

"I was only paid $40 a week, but the job gave me the illusion of wealth and independence. In exchange for squaring traffic tickets for the office staff, we had passes for every entertainment and sporting event. Liquor was free because the dry squads of the sheriff's office, the D.A.s, and the police competed in furnishing us with the best specimens of evidence from bootleggers. We dispensed important favors to judges. (In those days most judges were uncertain of re-election, and a stream of favorable news stories was the life-line to job security.) All this was heady stuff to a 22-year-old cub!" (RWK)

The study of law was a sideline suggested by a colleague who hoped to become a judge (and never did). The University of Southern California Law School was located close to the courthouse, and Kenny (now on the afternoon *Herald*) could get in an 8 and a 9 o'clock class without missing the day's action on his beat. Sometimes, when not much news was breaking, he could slip in an afternoon class as well. He broke no record for regular attendance, but as time went on, his interest deepened. Eventually, he enrolled in Loyola Law School to study Code Pleading under the distinguished Leon Yankwich* and began taking a daytime quiz course on the California Bar Exam under George Nix, "a blind attorney who knew every important California case book by heart and had memorized every important California code section. Between them, Yankwich and Nix made a lawyer out of me." (RWK)

After taking the Nix course twice, Kenny decided to try a practice shot at the Bar Exam. In view of his spotty and irregular legal education, he expected special scrutiny by the examiners and was prepared to repeat both the course and the

---

* THEN IN PRIVATE PRACTICE; later L.A. Superior Court judge, 1927–35, and then Judge, U.S. District Court from 1935 until his death in February, 1975.

The staff of the Daily Palo Altoan. *(Kenny in back row, right.)*

exam.   To his surprise, he passed the first time and was admitted to the California Bar on September 13, 1926.

"But this eminence had arrived before I was entirely ready. There was too much going on at that time, and as a courthouse reporter I was in the center of it. But my knowledge of the law stood me in good stead even though I delayed my entrance into the practice of it. It was the time of the Julian oil scandal, and one of my law courses had included the fact that when an indictment is returned by a grand jury, the defendants are entitled to a transcript of the hearings.

"There was a great deal of curiosity about what had been going on behind the closed doors of those hearings, and there were twenty-nine defendants, all entitled to a transcript. I arranged with one of them to take delivery on his volumes as soon as the grand jury's shorthand reporter had them completed. Another *Herald* reporter and I proceeded to digest the secret testimony, and for two days the *Herald* was filled with our exclusive summary of the disclosures.

"I don't know whether or not it was coincidental, but that was the last news story I ever worked on." (RWK)

In September 1927 Kenny was appointed deputy county counsel for Los Angeles County and for the next four years served in that capacity, first in Los Angeles and then in Sacramento, where he acted as a "sort of pioneer lobbyist" during the sessions of the state legislature, pushing bills of particular interest to his home region and pressing for appropriations needed for such projects as flood control and sewage treatment.

Kenny enjoyed the Sacramento stint more than he had expected. He learned how alliances and power blocs are formed, dissolved, and reformed in the whirlpools and eddies of a legislative session—experience that was to come in handy when he became a legislator himself. Also he met and worked with men doing chores similar to his for other regions and special interest groups. One of these was Earl Warren, who was lobbying on behalf of the law enforcement establishment.

"Warren and I worked together on a number of bills. One that I remember had to do with bail bonds. The bail-bond brokers had come up with a notion whereby if a man jumped his bail and left them to pay the forfeit, they would get their money back if the fellow turned up within three months. Warren said it was like 'giving a felon a leave of absence.' He and I did some fast footwork and defeated the bill for that session, but eventually our vigilance relaxed, and it got through." (RWK)

One of the side attractions of a county counsel's field work was the generous expense account considered essential for the persuasion of legislators. It enabled Kenny to "establish contact with old Stanford friends, now office holders in the state government, and to entertain former colleagues of the press. It got me acquainted with the people who were going to elect a governor next time up. And, as you may know, a judge is just a fellow who knew a governor." (RWK)

The people with whom Kenny became friendly that session were the organizers of the campaign of Jim Rolph, Mayor of San Francisco, who turned out to be the long-shot winner of the 1930 race. All three of the contenders were Republicans, so the crucial election was the primary. ("Winning the Republican primary in California in those days was as good a guarantee of eventual victory as winning a Democratic primary anywhere in the Solid South.") (RWK)

Kenny was not a registered Republican. (He declined to state any party affiliation until 1942.) What attracted him to Rolph was the non-partisan issue of repeal of the Prohibition Law, which Rolph was believed to favor. Deputy county counsels were not permitted to take an active part in any political campaign, but Kenny promised his friends in Rolph's press corps

that he would help as much as he could if he could find a way
to do so without getting into trouble.

"The big race in Los Angeles was between the two other candidates: Buron Fitts, the local district attorney; and the incumbent governor, Milton K. Young. Fitts was the candidate of the
drys* and of a radio preacher named Shuler, whom I heard one
night urging listeners to declare themselves by putting Fitts-for-
Governor stickers on the car windshields.

"It was a novel idea at the time, but it struck me as useful—
not for Fitts, who didn't need the publicity—but for our man,
Rolph. You see, there were a lot of people in Los Angeles who
were willing to vote for anyone so long as he could defeat the
Shuler-Fitts-Prohibition combination. They didn't care whether
it was Young or Rolph. What we needed to do was make it
look as if Rolph was a real contender, one who could beat Fitts
if he got a few more Los Angeles votes." (RWK)

To this end, Kenny (acting through a friend from one of the
press bureaus) hired a dozen attractive young movie extras and
posted them on street corners where traffic lights stopped cars
long enough for the "sticker girls" to work their powers of persuasion on drivers. "The depression was just beginning, and
these kids could use the $5 per afternoon as well as the chance
to be seen in public. With a smile and a pleasant word they could
vamp a Rolph sticker on to a Baptist preacher's car." (RWK)

Thus, for a relatively small investment, Kenny was able to
create the impression that Los Angeles was Rolph country. But
that was only half the battle. "In every campaign of this sort
there are actually two separate efforts: one is to elect your
candidate, and the other is to convince him that it was you who
did it." (RWK)

Fortunately, Carl Moritz, Kenny's friend in the inner circle,
was the press agent who usually accompanied Rolph on his campaign trips to Los Angeles, and another friend was the driver of
Rolph's official limousine. One or the other was usually able to
give advance warning of the route Rolph would be taking into
the city. Kenny would make sure that his sticker brigade was
working on cars going in the opposite direction. "You see
that?" Moritz or the driver would say to Rolph as they passed
the girls at work. "That's some of Bob Kenny's doing."

---

* DRYS AND WETS in this context are partisans or opponents of the Prohibition Amendment to the U.S. Constitution.

Rolph finished second in Los Angeles, and first, by 30,000 votes, over the whole state.

Soon after he took office, the legislature created a number of new superior and municipal judgeships in Los Angeles, all to be filled by gubernatorial appointment. "There wasn't a lot of competition among the Los Angeles lawyers to whom the new governor was favorably disposed. He had really been a long shot. Most of the Bar down here had come out for Fitts, who looked like a sure thing, or tried to stick with Governor Young." (RWK)

On August 20, 1931, Robert Kenny was appointed a municipal court judge. Not quite thirty years old, he had not practiced law for the required five years, but he persuaded the governor to post-date his commission to September 13, by which time he was able to qualify.

A few months later, Kenny was assigned by the presiding judge of the department to the Small Claims Court, a position which was not considered desirable. "I was being punished. It was partly for my espousal of the cause of Repeal (which was not illogical in view of the fact that most of the business transacted in our municipal courts had to do with enforcement of the Prohibition Law) and partly for another indiscretion: having voted for the man who came in second in the race for presiding judge." (RWK)

But the Small Claims Court turned out to be a gold-rich Siberia for an ex-newspaperman. No attorneys were permitted there. Controversy was served up raw. The sums of money involved were insignificant, so the press usually neglected to cover the proceedings. But Kenny found and exploited a vein of "human interest stories": cases involving pets—dogs, cats, snakes, birds, even alligators. His colleagues of the Fourth Estate knew a good thing when it was offered them, and soon Kenny's image was being presented several times a week to the animal-loving public.

Kenny also heard cases involving the shrinking or stretching of ladies' dresses by cleaners. He made it a rule that no claims for damages of this type would be honored in his court unless the plaintiff was willing to model the garment in court or in chambers, so that his Honor could determine the degree to which its fit had been distorted. Photographers found that sort of bait irresistible.

Behind this facade of unjudicial levity, Kenny was introducing changes in the functioning of the court that made it more useful to the segment of society it was designed to serve. When he first took over, the calendar was so crowded that citizens who brought an action—or were defending themselves against one—often had to sacrifice a whole working day. Kenny began by opening court an hour early. Then, as the popularity of small claims litigation kept pace with the enlarged calendar, he abolished first one, then the other half of the noon recess. He took to eating a sandwich and drinking a bottle of milk on the bench, which also made good news pictures. Finally, the court was sitting a full eight hours—unheard of before or after this time!—and no one had to wait more than an hour past the scheduled time of his/her case.

Another Kenny innovation of some importance was the tone he established and demanded from even the most bellicose litigants. In January 1932, only a few months after his appointment, he had a notice posted in the clerk's office which read:

TO LITIGANTS IN THE SMALL CLAIMS COURT

With the holidays over, I face the prospect of hearing about 20,000 small claims cases during the 1932 year. I hope that the litigants in this court will help me get through the year by observing the following suggestions:

1st, to forget all they have read about courtrooms being arenas, and lawsuits, battles in which everything is fair and no holds are barred;

2nd, to regard the small claims court as a place where two persons who may honestly disagree can submit their difference to a disinterested third person, remembering that in most lawsuits neither side is wholly right or wholly wrong;

3rd, to present only honest claims and defenses without quibbling;

4th, to remember that this court can only give judgement up to $50, and that while $50 is a lot more money than it used to be, it is not yet a matter of life and death;

5th, to present cases truthfully, but briefly, and to furnish the court light, not heat;

6th, to treat your opponent not as an enemy or a liar, but as another human being with whom you have a sincere disagreement over a question of law or fact;

7th, to stifle hatred and ill will, but if you must give vent to it, to aim it at the judge instead of your opponent. The judge is paid for that sort of thing, and if there must be ill will, it is better that it be focussed on him than diffused throughout the community;

8th, to indicate your willingness to accept these principles by offering to shake your opponent's hand when you are called before the judge to present your case.

I am not trying to be a Pollyanna judge, and I don't expect Clerk John Dugan or Bailiff Max Richman to be the Happiness Boys, but I am appalled at the prospect of hearing 20,000 petty, bickering lawsuits and neighborhood quarrels this year, with each side using every sort of unfair means to take advantage of the other. It is not unreasonable to ask litigants to adopt the attitude of sportsmanship toward each other. If they do, cases can be expedited and crowded calendars cleared. Expressions of personal animosity take up much of the time of this court that should be devoted to arriving at the truth.

Robert W. Kenny, Judge.

The results of this approach were not all that Kenny had hoped. While a few of the litigants were willing to shake hands on request, so many refused that it became embarrassing, and Kenny did not press the matter. Worse was what happened after judgement had been rendered. So many of the losers lurked outside the courtroom waiting to take a poke at the winners that the bailiff nicknamed the hall near the elevator bank, the Appellate Court.

Kenny decided that this situation was incompatible with judicial dignity and devised a strategem to cure it: he had his bailiff detain the loser for a few minutes after decision had been rendered to give the winner time to escape unscathed. Another tactic was to announce that "the Court will take the matter under advisement and send you a postcard." In such cases, both parties left the courtroom "happily confident of eventual victory; when the bad news came to the loser, he was at home or in his office and had only his family or fellow workers to tie into." (RWK)

Before long Kenny wisecracks had begun to make news, and people came to his court expecting to enjoy themselves. Courtroom laughter became such a problem that eventually he had to add another to his list of suggestions to litigants:

9th, Don't be provoked to anger when the audience laughs during your trial. Stick around and enjoy a few grins at the expense of the next victim.

The next time there was a vote for presiding judge of the department, Kenny's man won, and a few weeks later he was offered a reprieve from Small Claims. But Kenny chose to stay on until, in December 1932, Governor Rolph appointed him to the Superior Court.

Even here, Kenny found himself "still unable to adjust to no longer being a reporter on the beat. One afternoon during a murder trial, the district attorney switched the schedule of witnesses to be called. A few minutes after the reporters for the afternoon papers had left the courtroom, he suddenly decided to call to the stand the widow of the deceased! This was bound to be the highlight of the trial.

"Now, my loyalties were with the afternoon, as against the morning papers, and this surprise switch was more than my blood could bear. When the lady had given about ten minutes of her testimony, I called an adjournment, left the bench, phoned my old city editor, and dictated a new lead on the developments in the widow's testimony, in time to catch the final street edition. I then returned to the bench and the trial proceeded." (RWK)

Outside the court Kenny was devoting all his time to the campaign for the repeal of Prohibition. Young men of the same persuasion had formed a national organization called "The Crusaders," and Kenny became its California commander. In this capacity he "went about entering into wet-dry debates, usually pitted against Protestant clergymen. It was exciting and enjoyable. No one thought Prohibition would really be repealed, and it seemed we had an issue that would last us a lifetime. But it was also considered dangerous to a man's personal political hopes." (RWK)

Setting a pattern that was to last for his political lifetime, Kenny ignored the warnings. When the Crusaders organized a parade modeled on Mayor Jimmy Walker's New York "beer parade" (but entitled a "prosperity parade" in deference to the strong temperance sentiment in Southern California), Kenny agreed to participate. Then the temperance lobby went to work, and by the time the parade was ready to roll, he was the only local political figure who had withstood the pressure to drop out. It was true, of course, that he had not yet gone through the "learning experience" of an election campaign, having been appointed to all the offices he had held so far. But he knew that sooner or later he was "going to have to make it on my own charm—or merits—and this sort of thing was not supposed to increase either in the public mind." (RWK)

Kenny led off the parade, not on a white horse, but in a white Packard, courtesy of the owner of a local night club that was featuring Louis Armstrong and his band. "The entire group was mounted on a flat-bed truck and tootled away magnificently as we paraded through the streets of downtown Los Angeles." (RWK)

Soon afterwards a number of Democratic candidates for the up-coming election began declaring themselves in favor of Repeal, and it was whispered that some Republicans (including those running for top state office) were secretly on the same side. The Crusaders had sent out questionnaires to all candidates, "promising—or threatening—to reward those whose replies were acceptable, with our endorsement. We did not expect many replies." But to his astonishment, Kenny, whose name was signed to the covering letter, began to be sought out by candidates for Congress and the state legislature and asked for his support. "I found myself, at age 30, the only visible leader of a movement that was suddenly considered to have a chance of winning at the polls." (RWK)

In November 1932, Prohibition was voted down nationwide, two to one. California went 69 percent for Repeal. And Los Angeles, which was supposed to be "chemically pure and bone dry," turned out to be 68 percent wet!

"I was given credit in some quarters for being able to predict the political future, and perhaps that was the basic ingredient in the myth of my invincibility. Politics is mostly folklore and mythology, and my myth was in pretty good working order after that 1932 wet-dry campaign." (RWK)

The 1932 elections marked the debut of the Democratic Party as a serious contender for public office in California. "Be-

fore then, if you wanted your talents recognized and your abilities rewarded, you had to turn to the Republican Party because
that was the only place it was possible for such recognition to
have political consequences." (RWK) But having "declined to
state" for so long, Kenny decided to maintain his independence
of affiliation a little longer.

The 1934 election—the first in which he had to run for office—turned out to be the most violently contested in California
history. Upton Sinclair, author of many widely read muckrak-
ing novels*, resigned from the Socialist Party and registered as
a Democrat in order to run for the governorship. His book,
I, Governor of California, and How I Ended Poverty, laid out
a program for cutting the Gordian knot of the Depression—
poverty in the midst of plenty—by a system of "production
for use" instead of for profit. The public response was instant
and astonishing. At least 800 End-Poverty-in-California Clubs
sprang up throughout the state with hundreds of thousands of
earnest volunteer workers. Sinclair's program—which included
state-established consumer goods factories; "land colonies"
where food for all was produced communally; state support of
those unable to work; radical changes in the tax structure along
the general lines of the single-tax system; and the issuance of
state bonds to make up any fiscal deficiency—all this so terrified
conservative Democrats that they split nine ways and let Sinclair win the nomination and get on the November ballot as the
party's nominee for governor. He faced two opponents: Raymond Haight, who was running as a Progressive** and on his
own Commonwealth Party ticket; and Frank Merriam, the Republican incumbent.

"It made a tough choice. Most of the voters who were against
Merriam were scared of Sinclair. It was partly his talk about
ending poverty, which sounded like pure anarchy to our unso-
phisticated ears, and it was partly the extraordinarily dirty campaign that was waged against him.

"Haight had a chance. Merriam, who was lieutenant governor
when Rolph died suddenly, was the one who called out the
state militia to suppress the San Francisco general strike, so he

* e.g., *THE JUNGLE, THE BRASS CHECK*, and later, the Lanny Budd
series.
** THE FIRST PROGRESSIVE PARTY in American politics began as
a reform caucus inside the Republican Party. In California it had a long
tenure in power because of Hiram Johnson's personal charisma, exercised
first as governor of the state and later as its U.S. Senator.

was anathema to labor. Even William Randolph Hearst couldn't stomach him. Hearst would have supported Haight if he'd been willing to drop his Commonwealth label and just run as a Progressive. (Progressive was not a radical tag in California in those days; Commonwealth was.) But Haight wouldn't do it." (RWK)

As the campaign progressed, it began to appear that either Haight or Sinclair could beat Merriam if the other withdrew. They caucused, and Sinclair was almost persuaded to pull out. Kenny believed it was pressure from others on the ticket that kept Sinclair from yielding, "one of the others being Culbert Olson, who was elected to the state senate while Sinclair was being counted out." (RWK)

Meanwhile, in the non-partisan arena of the Superior Court contest, Kenny was battling six opponents. "Only one of them gave me much trouble. He was the one who told the *Los Angeles Times* that I had 'sought the support of union labor.' " (RWK) Union labor's support was hardly worth having in those days before political action committees, and in this particular election it would have been something of a handicap. In any case, Kenny had not sought it. What he had done was fall into a crude political trap.

He received a letter early in his campaign, written on the letterhead of a local union, inquiring about his labor record. He replied that he had not been on the bench long enough to have one, but he mentioned the fact (which should have been well known to any union official) that he had ruled in favor of the International Longshoreman's Association (AFL) in a recent waterfront dispute: the first time that the injunctive process had been used in California by, rather than against, a group of strikers.

"The shippers were housing their strikebreakers in a city warehouse on the docks, and the longshore attorney came into my court and said the city had no right to use public facilities as a boardinghouse for scabs. He said, 'I want a writ evicting them,' and I gave him one." (RWK)

The letter of inquiry was, of course, a ruse. Kenny's reply was turned over to the *Los Angeles Times,* which was already antagonistic to Kenny, probably because of a letter he had written the Sinclair campaign office, praising the level on which that campaign was being conducted. It was an unsolicited and probably a foolhardy gesture from a man who had his own election to worry about. Sinclair was being attacked by most men in public life not only as a "red," but also as a screwball. But

Kenny was disgusted by the vicious tactics that were being used to stop him, was moved to say so, and did.

The *Times* endorsed one of Kenny's six opponents, who lost in the primary. In November, Kenny's only competition was a man who had already been recalled from the same office for having accepted a gift from a receiver in bankruptcy. "I believe it was an overcoat, but not a vicuna one."* (RWK)

* THE REFERENCE IS to a scandal of the Eisenhower Administration in which Sherman Adams, one of the President's closest friends and advisors, was accused of taking a bribe from a Boston industrialist, in the form of a vicuna overcoat and other valuable considerations, and forced to resign.

3.

The Legend of Ancestral Wealth

PERHAPS THE MOST SIGNIFICANT THING ABOUT KENny's first campaign was the list of his sponsors. It included the American Civil Liberties Union; a phalanx of Republican bankers who had been friends of his father; Carrie Jacobs Bond, famous as the composer of the period's most beloved sentimental ballad, "The End of a Perfect Day"; and a representative of the Brewery Workers' Union.

His ability to pull votes from both ends of the political spectrum was the other "basic ingredient in the myth of Kenny's invincibility." His charisma for left-liberal voters was not hard to understand: he was outspokenly sympathetic to their position on the rights of labor, minorities, civil liberties, and collective, anti-fascist security. But his attraction for right-wingers was always puzzling. Some conservatives probably assumed that economic self-interest placed him on their side of the center, but the widespread belief that Kenny was heir to a banking fortune was actually another myth. As a banker, or even a banker's heir, he was a "near miss."

The legend of ancestral wealth was largely a product of the Kenny name, which first came into prominence in gold-rush San Francisco along with that of Bancroft. Young George Kenny and Hubert Howe Bancroft came west together in 1852 and opened what became a successful book and stationery store. They prospered, first in partnership and later in friendly competition.

Bancroft eventually went into publishing and thence into what he called "the literary industry"—i.e., the mass production of historical works about the American West. George Kenny did well enough on his own to build his family an imposing eight-sided mansion on San Francisco's Russian Hill, in which his son, Robert Wolfenden Kenny, was born. Melvina Van Wickle Kenny bore two more children and then died, and George Kenny went back to Buffalo, New York, in search of a substitute mother for his young brood. He courted and married Celia Bancroft Derby, the widowed sister of his former partner.

This marriage was highly successful from the viewpoint of the children and presumably also from that of the contracting parties, but the family fortunes declined. The octagonal house was sold to a new owner in 1879.* Young Robert Wolfenden inherited nothing more substantial than good connections and migrated, first to Los Angeles, and later (about 1890) to Tombstone, Arizona, to serve his apprenticeship as a banker.

It was in Tombstone that he met his future wife, Minnie Minerva Carleton, who seems to have been there on business connected with the dissolution of her first marriage (to a San Diego clothing dealer named Summerfield). When Mr. Summerfield, who was as unlucky in business as in matrimony, filed insolvency papers in Los Angeles in 1886, Mrs. Summerfield filed for permission to operate as a "sole trader"—an unusual legal procedure by which a woman could divest herself of responsibility for the debts of an insolvent spouse and go into business on her own.

All of this was considered "original" for a young lady of solid family in California in the last quarter of the 19th century. Her choice of a marriage partner had been unusual in the first place. There were few Jews in the state and even fewer mixed marriages. Divorce was all but unheard of. (Kenny was always puzzled about the way the Carleton–Summerfield divorce was obtained, there being no record of it in Los Angeles and some question as to whether a "territorial divorce" was legal at the time.) But the most remarkable aspect of Minnie Minerva's behavior was the way she set about earning the living Mr. Summerfield had failed to provide. She did not go home to her pious Methodist father, although he was sympathetic enough to stake her to the small capital needed for the venture she had in mind. Instead, she rolled up her leg-o'-mutton sleeves and went to work at the one profession for which her up-bringing had prepared her: the keeping of a clean, pleasant, domestic establishment.

* IT STILL STANDS at the corner of Green and Leavenworth Streets, dwarfed by high-rise apartments.

She opened a lodging house called The Potomac, on a quiet street, close to the financial center of Los Angeles where the sort of bachelor businessmen she wanted as clients had their offices. The Potomac prospered, and some time during the first four years of her independence, Mrs. Summerfield took time off to make the journey to Tombstone—either to acquire a divorce or to recover from the psychological strain of having got one elsewhere.

Not long after she returned to Los Angeles, Robert Wolfenden Kenny shifted his base of operations from the Bank of Tombstone to the Los Angeles National Bank, which was situated two blocks from The Potomac. There he took up residence. He and Minnie Minerva did not marry until 1896, and by the time their son, Robert Walker Kenny, was born in 1901, both parents were approaching forty years of age.

The baby weighed thirteen pounds and caused so much havoc getting himself born that the attending physicians, whose attention was directed primarily toward saving the mother's life, dislocated and permanently crippled the infant's right arm.

People who try to explain the unique in Bob Kenny's character frequently mention the effects of this birth injury, but they fail to agree on what those effects were. It did not affect his general health although it led him to find outlets for his energy that didn't depend on the possession of two good arms. It did not result in his becoming a recluse or an introvert. It may even have turned him in the opposite direction, encouraging an above-average gregariousness. But it must have had a discouraging effect on the relationship between young Bob and his father.

The elder Kenny was a serious amateur sportsman. When he was already suffering from the chronic illness that cut short his life, he had a boxing ring set up on the third story of his home, and a trainer from the Los Angeles Athletic Club came every morning to work out with him. Young Kenny couldn't spar or indulge in any other physical sport with his father. All the two could do together in this line was to go every Sunday to the baseball game at Washington Park.

Kenny Sr. was co-owner of the Los Angeles Pacific Coast League team and had a box, to which his son was permitted to invite his neighborhood cronies. "That made me very popular in certain circles and led me to organize the first integrated sand-lot team in California. It happened because there was a large Negro community near the house we lived in at the time, and three of the boys who played vacant-lot ball were black.

When I organized a team to challenge the 28th Street Stars, they were all on it. It was perfectly natural; no special point made one way or the other. In fact, I don't remember there being any of this anti-Negro or anti-Semitic thing in those days. I know I had to look up anti-Semitism in the encyclopedia the first time I heard the word, to find out what it meant." (RWK)

This managerial experience may have set Kenny's attitudes vis-à-vis minority groups. It certainly left him with a passion for baseball that continued, unabated, through his life. "This idea of challenging the 28th Street Stars was my father's. He had friends who lived in that neighborhood, which was considerably more fashionable than ours. Those kids even had uniforms! But my father said if I wanted to pit my sand-lot friends against them, he would lend me the ball park on a Saturday morning when it was not needed for regular practice.

"So I got up my team and put in the challenge.

"Actually the 28th Streeters were a hell of a lot better than we were. They'd had more experience. But not even those men in uniform had ever played on a diamond as big as the one in Washington Park. The distance from the mound to home plate was more than their pitcher could manage. Of course it was no better for ours. Neither of them had ever thrown a ball that far.

"Well, as I was sitting there watching all those fancy pitches landing short, I had a flash of genius. I realized that a catcher is always throwing to second, and that's twice as far as the pitcher has to throw. So I switched our battery! I put the pitcher behind the plate and the catcher on the mound. That's how we beat them!" (RWK)

About this time "things were beginning to click" for Robert Kenny, Sr., in the business world. The family acquired an Alco* (the most expensive car on the market), a cook, a second maid and a chauffeur, and a new house (with boxing ring). Robert Jr. was enrolled at the prestigious Harvard Military Academy. (A more unlikely candidate for military school would be hard to imagine, and it is something of a miracle that five years of that sort of hard labor did not drive young Bob into misanthropy or melancholia.)

On graduation at age ten, he and his mother and aunt went to Europe for the grand tour, but before it was completed, the elder Kenny became so ill that the travellers were called home. A year and a few months later, Robert Wolfenden Kenny died

---

* MADE BY THE American Locomotive Company.

from a mastoid infection of the type that would be easily treatable today.

"If Dad had lived a couple of more years—maybe five—I think he might have been very rich. He had a lot of things going for him. He and his friend, George Walker, from whom I got my middle name, had pioneered in oil properties up in Kern County. They had one near Yerba Linda, where Nixon was born. He had a piece of the Bank of Tucson and another of the Bank of Santa Monica, which I was told later on had been acquired with the idea of setting me up in business there. He was a partner of Harry Chandler's in the Tejon Ranch and other Mexican properties, and of course, there was that share of the Angel City ball club.

"But when he died, a lot of those things had to be sold to pay debts. One of the things that went was that Bank of Santa Monica stock, which is how I escaped being a banker. All in all, the estate netted down to about $100,000 for my mother and a third of that for me.

"The legend of my great affluence is really based on my relationship with George Walker, who was to go on and rack up some eight million dollars. The two families were very close. We always called each other uncle or aunt or whatever was appropriate, generation-wise. After my father's death, Uncle George looked after me. Of course a lot of my father's friends tried to help. That was how I got my first newspaper job on Chandler's *Los Angeles Times.* But the relationship with the Walkers was more than that. It was like real family." (RWK)

Kenny was executor of George Walker's will. The only heir was a daughter named Ethelwyn, who inherited the entire fortune on her father's death. Since she was childless, it was assumed by everyone that Robert Walker Kenny was next in line of succession. However, at some time in the late 1940s or early 1950s, Ethelwyn Walker Jarnigan was persuaded to make a different disposition of her inheritance.

"At some time during the period when I was all tied up with the Hollywood Ten case, a Mr. Otis Ivy, who was the brother of the president of the Citizens Bank, conducted a long and active courtship of Ethelwyn. A bank-presidential type of courtship, you understand, because Otis had a wife and Ethelwyn had an invalid husband. The result of this rapprochement and some unusually effective redbaiting was that Ethelwyn was induced to write a long, holographic will leaving the entire multi-million dollar package to Otis!

"When Ethelwyn died suddenly in 1952, I discovered that my great expectations were up the flue, and what was stickier, Jarnigan—the husband she probably expected to outlive—was left penniless! He was bedridden, poor fellow, and had to have nurses around the clock. I became his attorney (which, incidentally, meant that I had to resign from the Board of Directors of the Citizens Bank in order to bring suit on his behalf). We didn't dare go into court to try to break that will. It had one of those *in terrorem* provisions designed to scare the hell out of anybody who tries to break a will. But I did manage to get an allowance that maintained him.

"Those Ivy brothers must have scared poor Ethelwyn to death. Uncle George wouldn't have been susceptible to that sort of tactic. He was a Republican, of course, but he was a real independent thinker. And in those days you could dissent a little and not get pushed outside the pale. This terrible conformity hadn't descended upon us. You could be an advocate of free speech and still respectable, even among Republicans like Uncle George. It wasn't till F.D.R. died and the coalition fell apart that this thing developed where you not only had to agree with your friends, but you had to dislike the people they disliked." (RWK)

This background and these connections explain some of Kenny's ability to draw strength in the 1930s and '40s from the conservative sector of the Democratic Party even though he was speaking and acting for its left-liberal wing. They also explain the strains that developed in and finally destroyed his political base in the post-Roosevelt period. To a poor man who was a radical in politics, Kenny looked rich and his connections looked conservative. To his father's associates—the Walkers, the Chandlers, and other denizens of the California Club—he began by representing the farthest permissible extreme of liberalism. But the views of such men changed in the Truman era. The gap between their views and Kenny's widened until "Bob Kenny's boy, Bob" began to look, even to George Walker's daughter, Ethelwyn, like a renegade recruit to the cause of the proletariat.

4.

Into the Arena

URING MOST OF HIS TERM ON THE SUPERIOR COURT (1932–8) Kenny refused to state any party affiliation although he did become the chairman of the Southern California Committee of Progressives for Roosevelt. Organization Democrats accepted whatever assistance this splinter group could offer, but "they were becoming impatient with those who were still afraid to be Democrats although we were ashamed to be Republicans." (RWK)

Roosevelt's overwhelming electoral victory in 1936 put the California wing of his party in control of the state assembly for the first time in most voters' memory. From this vantage point the Democrats were able to open an investigation into corruption in the state government and "the entrenched Republican machine began to develop some bad knocks." (RWK)

By the fall of 1937, the campaigns for governor and the legislature were opening. Democrats sensed the possibility of winning on all levels. Culbert Olson announced his candidacy for the governorship on the Democratic ticket. Kenny agreed to be treasurer of Olson's Los Angeles organization and decided to file for the state senate seat Olson was vacating.

Forced at last to register as a Democrat, Kenny had some trouble breaking the habits acquired as a "decline-to-stater." Early in the campaign he committed what regulars considered a serious breach of party discipline. He endorsed Earl Warren, who was running for attorney general and cross-filing on the Democratic primary ballot.

The left-labor forces that made up one wing of the Democratic Party were hostile to Warren because of his role as the prosecutor who had sent union leaders Earl King, E.G. Ramsay, and Frank Connor to jail in the *Point Lobos* case—one of several

instances of violence in the aftermath of the San Francisco
general strike of 1934. The three men were convicted of com-
plicity in the fatal beating of a waterfront strikebreaker. Warren
was accused by the Left of having railroaded them to jail in exchange for the political backing of the shipowners. (Nothing in
the trial record reflected discredit on Warren's integrity, but his
obstinate refusal to consider clemency kept the resentment alive
during his tenure as governor, and it is interesting that his last
official act before leaving that position to become Chief Justice
of the U.S. Supreme Court was to pardon the last of the *Point
Lobos* defendants.)

Kenny knew Warren and considered him "a model prosecutor
in a very tough district and a good government man." So when
Fletcher Bowron (later Mayor of Los Angeles) asked Kenny to
endorse Warren, he said he'd consider it.

"A luncheon was arranged, and I told Warren I thought I understood his position on the *Point Lobos* case, but I was going
to need some help making my civil liberties friends understand
it. He said he'd send me the trial record, and he did. I read it
through and found nothing to indicate that he had acted out of
prejudice. What was more important, he also sent me a long
handwritten statement of his views on the guarantees of the Bill
of Rights.* It was really very impressive when you consider the
time it was written and the political climate in California.

"So I endorsed him. He used the letter in his campaign, and
that made our conversation public and brought down on my
head the avalanche of Democratic wrath. The Hollywood Central Young Democrats excoriated me and said they weren't
going to support me. Tom Mooney wrote me from San Quentin
saying he was going to withdraw the Mooney vote!

"I saved that letter of Warren's. It enabled me almost fifteen
years later to predict with astonishing accuracy the sort of Chief
Justice he was going to make. I was the only one of those who
rushed into print with a prediction, to point the direction in
which Warren was turning. Even Ike, who made the appointment, had no such prescience.

"I've sometimes wondered what would have happened if I
hadn't endorsed Warren. He wasn't known in our end of the
state, especially among our people. He really needed help from
some maverick Democrat like me. You have to be careful in

* cf. Appendix A.

politics about who you give a leg up to. Sometimes the fellow ends up standing on your neck." (RWK)

The importance to Warren's career of Kenny's endorsement in this, Warren's first campaign for state-wide office, cannot be underestimated. It was a year of Democratic landslides everywhere. Warren's only chance was to win a place on the Democratic ticket while the real Democrats were busy fighting each other.

The campaign he waged for the nomination was so "nonpartisan" that some people claim he got through the whole contest without mentioning anything more controversial than the desirability of lawful order in the land. But even so, he had to look like a Democrat to Democrats when it came time to mark the primary ballot. He needed some evidence that Democratic office-holders considered him acceptable. Kenny was the one who provided the evidence.

As for Kenny's own campaign, it was inexpensive and "speechless." Neither the wrath of the Young Democrats of Hollywood nor that of the Mighty Man of San Quentin affected its outcome. He won in a walk.

"Of course the state senate was just a joke job at that time— before the 'one man, one vote' decision. The sole state senator from Los Angeles County couldn't do anything but minor repairs and maintenance work because all of us city senators were too badly outnumbered by the boys from the back counties.

"But I thought I'd been a judge long enough. I wanted to throw my weight around on things that interested me." (RWK)

During the legislative term (1938–1942), Kenny threw his weight around with an élan that left observers gasping. And when he wasn't working, he was playing with the same frenetic intensity.

Always gregarious, he began to surround himself with a wildly assorted group of allies, admirers, and sycophants. He indulged his passion for betting on the races whenever he could get to the track. He played the pinball machines in Sacramento saloons, drank with the boys, and kept his ear tuned to the oracles of rumor.

One of the most persistent rumors of that session was that the Kenny marriage was breaking up. By the end of Bob's second year in the senate, Sara Kenny was seen so rarely at of-

Robert and Sara Kenny.

ficial functions that explanations had to be made, the most common being that she was participating in some "retreat" or other activity connected with the Baha'i faith, to which she was a convert. What seemed harder to explain was why this odd mismatch had come about in the first place.

Sara McCann was one of the most beautiful co-eds of her day at Stanford—intelligent though not brilliant, shy, introverted, and deeply religious. Bob was as different as it was possible to be in all respects except intelligence. (Sara confessed years later that it was Bob's "enormous erudition" that first attracted her.) He was boisterously sociable, something of a campus cut-up, owner of the only Stutz Bearcat on the Stanford parking lot, a skeptic in religion, and so painfully conscious of his disability that as far as his fraternity brothers knew, he had never dated a girl until he turned up in his senior year engaged to the glamorous Miss McCann.

How that conquest was achieved was a mystery that baffled those who knew the couple best. Before long the mystery that concerned both of the principals was not how, but why. One man who was devoted to both Bob and Sara told me the underlying problem was not simply their differences. "There was no common interest between them. Nothing! No timber to build a bridge. They were always courteous to each other and helpful when they could be. I think Sara wanted to divorce him some time during that senate term, but it would have hurt his campaign for attorney general, so she didn't. And Bob took a dim view of her religion, but he never made an issue of it.

"Of course, Sara used to get mad at some of the things Bob was doing and you couldn't blame her."

The things Bob was doing were drinking to excess and tomcatting—both occupational diseases of a politician's life that we have come to accept in the post-Watergate era of total exposure. Kenny's case was probably no more acute than the average. If his drinking was more public than that of most legislators, that was regarded as a function of the "Kenny style" of refusing to put a pious face on things.

What Sara recalled as the galling disappointment of her early married life was her distaste for the world in which her husband had decided to make his way. Knowing nothing about politics, she decided it was her duty to acquaint herself. So day after day, week after week, she attended all the open sessions of both houses of the legislature and all committee hearings.

"I listened to what they were saying and I couldn't believe it! So I listened some more. And I was disgusted. Just disgusted! At this *trash* that was supposed to be representing the people. Making laws! Governing!

"And what Bob could see in them was even more unbelievable. They weren't his kind of people. But they fawned on him, hoping for favors, and he seemed to enjoy it."

Less and less able to understand or to influence Bob, Sara turned more and more to her religion. Heavier and more fulfilling responsibilities were laid upon her by her fellow Baha'is, and soon she was building the foundation of what was to be a separate life.

What Sara Kenny failed to perceive through the smog of Bob's flamboyant misbehavior was the solid accomplishment of his four years as a senator. No matter how high the carouse of the night, Kenny was at work next morning before most of his colleagues were up and shaved.

Ewing Haas, who was bill clerk of the legislature that term, remembered that Kenny would turn up at the door of the Bill Room when it was still locked.

"We'd be busy preparing the books that go on the members' desks each day: the histories and the journals and all that stuff. We'd hear Kenny's knock. We knew it, and we always let him in.

"He'd get at one end of the long counter we had down there and pick up copies of every bill that had been introduced or amended or whatever. He could look at a page—just scan it!— and tell you what was on it. I've watched him make notes at the top of all those bills at seven in the morning when maybe he'd been to bed and maybe he hadn't. The notes he was making were for his staff: things like 'Send this to so-and-so' or 'What's-his-name would be interested in the later amendment on this one' and so on.

"When his staff showed up at the regular hour, all the material would be there for them to work on, and Kenny would be back at his hotel, showering or napping. He was one senator who knew what was in the bills. He read them. All of them!"

Many of them he wrote.

There is a story still current in Sacramento that Bob Kenny introduced so many bills during his first week in the senate that the opposition never got off the ground with its plan for that session. That may be hyperbole, but he did introduce forty-six bills on his first day, and that was more than half the total introduced by all other senators during the term.

Most of Kenny's proposals were voted down by his peers or vetoed by the governor, but many eventually did become law when the collective mind of the legislature caught up with his. In the meantime, he continued to take so highly visible a stand on unpopular issues he considered important that he came to be known as the "lone no-vote" man in the senate.

He was, for example, the only opponent to a bill outlawing the Communist Party. His tactic was not to speak against the measure, but to propose an amendment, providing that the party should be removed from the ballot only after a hearing before the secretary of state, in which cause could be shown and counterarguments adduced. "My amendment was voted down by the excited patriots in the state senate, but it would have made their bill constitutional. When the roll was called, I cast the solitary no vote, and the next year the State Supreme Court unanimously struck down the measure on the ground that due process was denied because no hearing was provided." (RWK)

Among the measures Kenny pushed at every session during his term was one outlawing capital punishment. (It took until 1972 for the California State Supreme Court to catch up with him on that issue. But when Kenny became attorney general in 1942, he asked for and got a law that forbade the posting of "dead or alive" rewards for wanted fugitives, a practice which had operated as a sort of extra-legal capital punishment in a number of instances.)

The salary of a state senator in California in 1938 was a munificent $100 a month. Kenny had to practice law in Los Angeles to stretch this sum to cover living expenses, and to that end he entered into partnerships, first with a president of the state bar, later with other attorneys.

As eclectic in his choice of clients as he was in his choice of friends, Kenny had at one time the cases of a Republican member of the State Board of Equalization, who was defending himself against a charge of having mishandled liquor licenses, and William Schneiderman, chairman of the Communist Party of California, who was fighting an effort to revoke his citizenship.

"On one occasion when they happened to drop into the office at the same time, I introduced them to each other. The Republican and the Communist got along very well. However, this sort of behavior on my part confused Governor Olson, to whom everything had to be either black or white. He once wrote Carey McWilliams complaining about me, that I was as much at home with reactionary Republicans as I was 'in fraction meetings of the Communist Party.' It was not the first or the last time a lawyer would have attributed to him the politics of his clients." (RWK)

In the spring of 1942, State Senator Robert W. Kenny announced that he would oppose Governor Culbert Olson in the gubernatorial primaries that year.

Strains between Kenny and Olson had developed even before the end of the 1938 campaign, and during the three years of

Olson's incumbency they had grown so intense that it was impossible to conceal them for the sake of party unity. The differences between the men were both political and personal.

Kenny was a liberal with no commitment to a socialist solution to any of the state's problems; Olson was a socialist of the Upton Sinclair school—reformist, rather than revolutionary, and increasingly anti-Communist. On the subject of ethical standards the two held diametrically opposite views. Olson's private life would have passed muster in circles were Kenny was considered a roué. But Kenny's political integrity was absolute while Olson recognized "the necessity of resorting to questionable means to achieve righteous ends."

Twenty years later, Justice Philip Gibson, one of Olson's principal lieutenants at the time, not only made the above mildly ironic apology, but still complained that "Bob Kenny seemed unable to understand the governor's very real problem about rewarding hungry Democrats with patronage jobs."

The problem was indeed a real one. Olson was the first Democrat in a position to dispense that sort of largesse in over fifty years. But he had been elected as a reform candidate and was expected to clean out the corruption in state government against which he had inveighed. It was perhaps impossible in the circumstances to satisfy everyone, but Olson ended up satisfying no one.

After three years in office, he was considered to have "betrayed" a sizable section of the regular Democratic organization in the matter of employment, and it was generally agreed that his administration was at least as corrupt as the one it had replaced. Kenny, who was not involved in any of the Sacramento scandals, was putting together what he later called "a coalition of the disaffected," and what little in the way of a "machine" Olson had managed to put together was considered no match for it.

Most political commentators predicted that Kenny would carry the primaries and go on to win in November against the only Republican candidate on the horizon—Attorney General Earl Warren, who had not yet even declared. And some, looking even farther into the future, were predicting that Kenny was a front-runner for the nomination as Roosevelt's running-mate in the 1944 elections. There was no doubt that Roosevelt was going to be nominated for a fourth term, and little doubt that he was looking for a new Vice President. (It was said that he wanted a different sort of man managing the Senate when treaties came before it for ratification at the war's end.) With Henry Wallace out of the picture, there was every reason to choose a westerner "to balance the ticket." Kenny, as governor of the biggest west coast state, would head his delegation to the Democratic National Convention, probably as its favorite son candidate, and his extraordinary record of political victories would also recommend him to the slate-makers.

The difference it would have made in the political climate of post-World War II America if Robert W. Kenny, rather than Harry S. Truman, had been Vice President in April 1945 is enough to jolt the confidence of those who deny the importance of the individual in the making of history.

But Kenny was not elected governor of California in 1942. He did not run. And the decision to withdraw from the race before it was well started was a measure of how deep Kenny's antagonism to Olson had become.

Kenny blamed Olson for using his services during the campaign and snubbing him after inauguration day. "It may have all started when the *Los Angeles Times* ran an editorial that predicted I was going to be the Grand Poo-Bah of the new administration. Some people thought the term referred to a sort of sexual deviant. But I doubt that Olson was that ignorant of the works of Gilbert and Sullivan. What's more likely is that it made him suspicious that I had intentions of manipulating him as Ko-Ko was manipulated by Poo-Bah." (RWK)

It was certainly not hard to make the new governor suspicious. His distrust of the "non-orthodox" extended all the way from Earl Warren Republicans to the conservative members of his own Democratic Party.

There was an unpleasant incident half-way through his term when it was discovered that a microphone had been planted behind the valance over the window of the hotel room occupied by a Democrat who had just been elected speaker of the state assembly. There was a flurry of indignant protest, and some talked of a recall of Olson, who was believed responsible for this and other instances of illegal surveillance. When Kenny was asked if he supported such a move, he said he hadn't decided whether he was for recalling the governor, but he certainly wished the governor could recall him.

The pun was costly. It made public the estrangement between the two men, and on Olson's side, probably made it irreversible. He was utterly without humor and did not tolerate wit in his associates. But Kenny was in no mood to play the diplomat. He considered himself a wronged man.

According to Justice Raymond Peters, who was party to the machinations which in the end "kept Bob Kenny from sitting on the California State Supreme Court as everyone expected him to," it was no secret throughout the campaign that two of Olson's most important lieutenants wanted the same reward for their efforts: a place on the state's highest court. One of these was Bob Kenny; the other was Jesse Carter, who had been district attorney of Shasta County and one of the first governors of the State Bar. Not generally known was the fact that Olson's friend and advisor, Philip Gibson, also wanted such an appointment.

Immediately upon taking office, Olson rewarded Carter and Gibson, the former with an appointment to the state senate to fill a vacancy caused by death; the latter to the post of State Director of Finance. Kenny received no accolade so he was considered front-runner when a vacancy on the Supreme Court was created by the death of Justice Emmett Sewell in July 1939. (Kenny was, incidentally, the only one of the aspirants who had any experience on the bench.)

A delegation of Carter's friends, including Justice Peters, went to Olson to press their man's claims, and Olson explained his obligation to Kenny. He also said there was some question as to the eligibility of either Carter or Kenny since California law might be construed to bar the appointment of anyone holding elective office. The governor suggested that Kenny and Carter decide between themselves who should get the Sewell vacancy and file suit to get an eligibility ruling. In any case, Olson said, there would be other such openings in the future. It was simply a matter of "who first?"

Carter went to Los Angeles and talked with Kenny—an interview which was the start of a long, cordial friendship. (Kenny was later editor of an annotated collection of Carter's judicial opinions.) The upshot of the conversation was that both men called on Olson and asked him to appoint Carter to the Supreme Court and Kenny to a vacancy on the Los Angeles Appellate Court, as a stepping stone to Kenny's appointment to the high court at the first available opportunity. Pending the ruling on Carter's eligibility, both men would stay in the state senate.

Olson announced the Carter appointment, and the eligibility suit was filed. Kenny's appointment was understood (at least by him) to be delayed pending the decision on Carter's case. In

August, another Supreme Court justice died, and Olson immediately filled the vacancy with a surprise nominee: Philip Gibson. Five days later the State Supreme Court ruled that Carter (and therefore Kenny) was eligible. Kenny considered Olson's precipitant choice of Gibson the betrayal of an agreement, and he informed the governor that he was not available for the appellate court post. (Late in his term Olson appointed Kenny to an appellate court post anyway in what was generally considered a move to discourage him from opposing Olson in the Democratic primary. Kenny called the appointment a "mouse-trap" and turned it down.)

The results of this wrangle were bad for both combatants and for the commonwealth. Olson lost the support of a sector of his party without which he could neither govern effectively nor win re-election. Kenny's political ambition was diverted from the judiciary, where he could hardly have failed to attain a "good eminence," and focussed on replacing Olson as governor. And the state of California lost the services of a potentially great Supreme Court justice.

Not long after Kenny's announcement of his intention to run for governor, Earl Warren declared that he too would seek the office, not only on his own party's ticket, but also on the Democratic. In those days of cross-filing in California political contests, there were considerable advantages to such a maneuver. A candidate who won nomination on both tickets did not have to run in the fall. One who lost on his own (declared) ticket was eliminated even if he should win on the opposition's. But one who won on his own and lost on the other (as Warren was expected to do) had made a start at wooing votes from the other side in November. For Republicans, who were "outregistered" by Democrats, this was particularly important.

"Warren was playing good practical politics. He had already started going after Democratic votes when he ran for attorney general by using the 'non-partisan' approach. It made him the only Republican who got elected to a state office in that 1938 (Democratic) landslide, and he'd been careful to keep that nonpartisan image because he was going to need it in the final elections." (RWK)

Assessing the situation created by Warren's announcement, Kenny decided that if he and Warren both ran, they might split the anti-Olson vote and let the governor "coast in for another term. That was something I certainly didn't want to see happen. So I began to look around for alternatives, such as, for instance, the office Warren would be vacating to run." (RWK)

That office was generally referred to as "the second in the state," but it had not amounted to much until Warren took it over. According to Kenny, Warren had set his sights on it long before the incumbent (another Republican) "made any noises about retiring, and determined to remodel it for his future occupancy.

"Warren was D.A. of Alameda County at the time and heading up a sort of informal lobby of other D.A.s and peace officers over the state. With their help he got an amendment to the state constitution that made the attorney generalship into a sort of executive bureau directing all law enforcement. It also raised the A.G.'s salary to whatever was currently being paid associate justices of the State Supreme Court." (RWK)

All this considered, Kenny decided the attorney general's office was a good pied-à-terre for the next four years. But he had a problem about getting his hat out of the gubernatorial ring with reasonable grace.

"What I needed was a 'Draft Kenny' movement. Well, the Olson people didn't want me running against their candidate, so all of a sudden party regulars who had always hated me discovered virtues they had failed to perceive. They signed a paper begging me to run for the attorney generalship 'in the interests of unity.' When enough people signed, I graciously consented. I was thus able to get my hat out of one ring and into the other in a single motion." (RWK)

Kenny was willing to concede with the wisdom of hindsight that this dextrous maneuver may have been the greatest miscalculation of his career. "I didn't realize just how much anti-Olson sentiment there was. I could have won the Democratic primary even with Warren in there, and I might very well have gone on to beat him in November." (RWK)

5.

General Kenny and Governor Warren

THE CAMPAIGN KENNY WAGED IN 1942 WAS CONSIDERably less casual than his 1938 effort. He sought and made good use of a team of sponsors that covered all the bases: from the former Republican State Chairman, to the incumbent Democratic State Chairman; from the old Republican party hack who had been attorney general before Warren and the old guard Republican U.S. Senator, to the leaders of the State Federation of Labor and the C.I.O.

One political editor commented wryly that "the left-wingers evidently think he is not nearly so conservative as his conservative friends believe he is, while the conservatives consider him much less liberal than the left-wingers possibly hope he is. Which, after all, is just about the public impression most politicians are striving persistently to create."

The November elections in California reversed the results in 1938. Although Roosevelt had been re-elected on the national ticket, a solid bank of Republicans took over all the state offices except that of attorney general. Robert Kenny's stature, as the only Democratic holder of state office in the state with the largest number of electoral votes west of the Mississippi, was suddenly visible even from the Potomac. The next time Kenny visited Washington, he was summoned into the Roosevelt presence.

"He asked me about Warren. He said 'What kind of a fellow is your new governor out there?' I told him, 'Everything we have out there is better than it is anywhere else. Even our Republicans are part Democrat.' " (RWK)

Kenny attacked his new job with zest. He found it considerably more challenging than a seat in the state senate, and he enjoyed his position as the sole minority member of an administration "faced with the dismaying prospect of having to make good on campaign promises." His relations with the Warren regime were cordial. He found it easy to get the governor's cooperation on most of the projects he initiated, and bore none of the responsibility for the overall performance of the state government.

"I developed the position that the attorney general was the most mobile officer in the state," Kenny said, "one who could move in any direction, enter just about any matter." His special deputy, Charles Johnson (later a judge in Sacramento), put it even more strongly: "Kenny thought the office was delightful because nobody expected you to do anything, but you could go out and get into anything you wanted to. And we got into everything!"

"Everything" in this context meant whatever could be subsumed under the rubric "poor administration of justice." One example of this extension of the traditional field of operation for the attorney general's office was Kenny's assault on the exploiters of migrant labor through an "investigation of reports of police brutality in the treatment of migrant prisoners held in rural jails." Another and more daring extension was an examination of the legality of restrictive (housing) covenants.

This was a practice that permitted property owners in a "Caucasian" neighborhood to preserve their ethnic homogeneity by keeping non-Caucasians from owning, renting, or occupying a dwelling (except as servants). Once such an agreement was reached between incumbent owners, if a non-Caucasian moved in anyway, the covenanters could go to court and get an injunction against the "invasion." The matter had been tested in the state courts, which upheld such injunctions on the grounds that, while the Fourteenth Amendment to the U.S. Constitution might prevent a state from entering into such a discriminatory agreement, there was nothing to prevent individuals from doing so.

Kenny had found an article in a law review, written by a University of California professor named D.O. McGovney, that took a different view of the matter. McGovney argued that as soon as a state intervened to enforce a private contract, it became a state action—which put the Fourteenth Amendment back into effect.

"I decided that since I was attorney for the state, I was obligated to let the state courts know that I didn't believe they

Attorney General Kenny with Governor Earl Warren (left) and March of Dimes campaigner Stanley Pierson (right), 1946.

should be violating the federal constitution." (RWK) Kenny hired Professor McGovney to put his article into the form of a brief and submitted it to the State Supreme Court. The argument failed to win the necessary four-vote majority there, but the matter ultimately reached the U.S. Supreme Court, which ruled in favor of the Kenny-McGovney position. Restrictive covenants disappeared from the real estate broker's lexicon.

Another acre of new ground broken by Attorney General Kenny was segregation in the public school system. He directed the preparation of a brief, *amicus curiae,* in a suit challenging the practice of separating Mexican-American from Anglo-American children in Orange County schools. This effort also lost in the lower courts but won in the U.S. Court of Appeals.

Of all the briefs to which Kenny's name was signed during his term, he was proudest of these two. "Of course I didn't write either of them. That's the difference between the writing game and the law. In one case an editor gets no credit for the final product; the author gets it all, no matter who suggested the idea or helped him develop or polish it. In the other case, the man who sweats it out gets none of the credit; it all goes to the 'one who directed it to be written,' for having had the notion in the first place and editing it in the last." (RWK)

When he was not prospecting for new territory, Kenny was at work on the structure of his office and its staff, finishing the task that Warren had begun: weeding out the "ineducables and incompetents who were hold-overs from the days when the post of deputy attorney general was bestowed as a reward for political favors done or anticipated." (RWK) Kenny turned the office into a professional, non-political arm of government by a combination of shrewd, but diplomatic reshuffling of responsibility and the setting of an example that raised the quality of every subordinate's performance.

For instance, Kenny made it a practice to review all decisions made by his deputies—something not even the diligent Warren had attempted. This task increased the work load past the point where most men could have handled it, but Kenny was a natural speed-reader and enjoyed this test of his ability.

When he finally had the department functioning as he thought it ought to, Kenny persuaded his old colleagues in the legislature to pass a bill bringing the entire attorney general's office staff (with the exception of chief deputy) under civil service. Warren signed the measure into law with some reluctance, but he later became so convinced of the soundness of the arrangement that he was glad to claim credit for it as part of his own legislative program.

In this and many similar circumstances, Kenny and Warren worked well as a team despite their different political philosophies. Warren, the conservative, understood the kind of problems faced by Kenny, the liberal, as the lone minority member of a highly partisan administration because he, Warren, had sat very recently in the same hot seat. Also, Warren recognized not only that he owed Kenny a debt of political gratitude, but also that there was much he could learn from his brilliant young associate—much that Warren needed to learn if he was going to function effectively as governor and run for re-election, quite possibly against the same man.

This period in the relationship between Earl Warren and Robert Kenny has been the subject of serious scrutiny from the perspective of the ultimate political fate of the two men.

Many Californians, contemporaries in a position to observe Warren before and after the four years in which he worked closely with Kenny, believe that the latter was the root cause of the change in Warren that astonished most Republicans, including Dwight Eisenhower, who appointed him to the U.S. Supreme Court and is believed to have regretted it—a change from the political philosophy (or lack of one) that made the young district attorney of Alameda County acceptable to the reactionary Knowland machine,* to a system of judicial views that impelled right-wing Republicans to join with Southern Democrats in a call for his impeachment as a dangerous radical in high office.

One man who made such an assessment was Justice Raymond E. Peters,** who practiced law in the courts of Alameda County when Warren was district attorney there. "He was a vigorous—not to say a vicious!—prosecutor. And in the Supreme Court he emerged as a public defender! It was simply astonishing."

More so when one considers that Warren had no judicial experience in the intervening years from which he might have learned new perspectives. He had, in fact, no judicial experience at all before his elevation to Chief Justice. "But he did spend four years as governor, working a few doors down the hall from Kenny" who was in Peters' opinion "one of the brightest legal minds in the state, one that had been educated not only in the fundamental law, but also in the philosophy behind the law."

That impact took some thirty years to make itself felt. But Kenny's effect on Warren in the field of legislation was apparent to some observers in the second year of their collaboration. Carey McWilliams, writing in *The Nation* in 1943, noted "Warren's surprising ability to imitate and in some cases anticipate Kenny's genuine liberalism."

This was in sharp contrast to Warren's previous track record as a law-maker. Justice Peters' estimate of that record was that "Warren was responsible for some of the most conservative law ever passed in this state. For instance, he helped draft and then lobbied for our monstrous statute that makes it a felony to conspire to commit a misdemeanor. It's a legal absurdity, but it's an easy way to get convictions, and that's what the D.A.s wanted. As head of their association, Warren saw to it that they got it."

---

* THE OAKLAND REPUBLICAN organization headed by Joseph Knowland, publisher of the *Oakland Tribune*.
** JUSTICE RAYMOND E. PETERS was appointed to the California State Supreme Court in March 1959 and served there until his death in 1973.

Corroboration of the same thesis came from Robert Powers, who served as "general manager of law enforcement," first under Warren and then under Kenny. According to Powers, "the key to Kenny's influence on Warren was courage. Warren was honest—a very honest man—but he had never lived on the plane of courage that was natural to Kenny. Warren never did an incautious thing in his life, and Kenny rarely did a cautious one. Watching Kenny operate, Warren learned.

"Take the Japanese thing—sending all those families into concentration camps after Pearl Harbor. Warren looked bad. We all looked bad. We were all racists—except Kenny!

"I can say that about Warren because I say it about myself. I was a tough racist cop. But I learned. Most middle-class people in this country are mildly racist. Some of them know it and wish they could improve. But they don't dare make the move on their own.

"Then one brave man stands up. A Kenny, for instance. A man like Warren watches and sees that he doesn't have to be so timid after all. And he begins to change. It's the X factor of influence, the effect of courage. When you see it in action—strong, affirmative action!—it begins to look perfectly normal to you, and it's easy to follow the example."

6.

The Prophylactic Approach to Law Enforcement

THE BACKGROUND FOR POWERS'S OBSERVATION WAS Warren's—and later Kenny's—handling of the problem of what to do about the large west coast population of first-, second-, and third-generation Japanese-Americans at the time the Japanese air force bombed the chief U.S. naval base at Pearl Harbor.

Anti-Japanese sentiment had long been a feature of California politics. In December 1941, it was at a low ebb. There were, however, a number of organizations dedicated to keeping it at flood, all still active and looking for a chance to make their influence felt. The most important was the California Joint Immigration Committee, which Kenny characterized as "not a committee of any other body except the readership of the Hearst press, and 'joint' only in sense that it was bunch of guys joined together to persecute the Japanese."

In the days when inveighing against the "Yellow Peril" was an indispensible ingredient of any successful political campaign in California, the Joint Committee was a potent section of the right-wing coalition that controlled the state apparatus. It was made up of delegates from the American Legion, the State Federation of Labor, the State Grange, and the Native Sons of the Golden West. Earl Warren was an active member of the first and last of these organizations all his political life.

Within days after the Japanese attack on Pearl Harbor, proposals to evacuate the entire west coast Japanese-American population began to be heard in meetings of groups represented in the Joint Committee. In his capacity as attorney general, Warren was asked to appear before the Joint Committee in January 1942 and he spoke in favor of evacuation. "A more political approach" to whatever danger these people might represent was, he said "just too cumbersome. It is involved with too much red tape for us to do anything to protect our situation now. We are likely to get it before this day ends; we don't know. We are fighting against an invisible deadline."

Kenny was in the state senate where he was part of a majority bloc "that did manage to sidetrack the first wave of anti-Japanese resolutions. Most of them came from a wild man named Jack Metzger, from Red Bluff. He got some support, but not much.

"Later on, we had to listen to speeches by people like one Presbyterian minister I remember, who testified that after prayer and fasting he had concluded it was our Christian duty to keep the Japanese out of the western world! He was for deporting them right off the continent!"

The force behind these hysterical utterances in Kenny's opinion was "a deliberate propaganda campaign, emanating from the Hearst editorial offices, that was driving the populace into a frenzy of fear. People were reading those nutty Hearst headlines about arrow-shaped forest fires pointing the way to our cities, spies standing on the sand dunes flashing mirrors at submarines and so forth, and they got so jumpy they couldn't read their own radar. Why, one night in February [1942] somebody in Los Angeles picked up a false signal from a weather balloon, and we had a whole night of ack-ack." (RWK)

On February 19, 1942, Roosevelt signed Executive Order 9066, authorizing the military to take any action it found necessary to meet the internal threat. Two days later the Select Committee Investigating National Defense Migration [sic] was set up by the 77th Congress under the chairmanship of a California congressman named John Tolan.

The Tolan Committee opened hearings in San Francisco and invited the testimony of Attorney General Warren, who appeared with maps, prepared by his office, of Japanese-held lands. Warren pointed out to the committee members that "the disturbing situation" revealed Japanese farmers "within a grenade throw" of defense plants, coastal defense guns, beaches, air fields, railroads, power lines, gas and water mains.

Historians writing after what Kenny called "the sobering up from this racist binge" have found it hard to believe that Warren was not aware of the reasons for this strange state of affairs: that the Japanese farmers who settled in California in the early years of this century had been too poor to afford any but the cheapest land, sage brush desert or the barren hills south of Los Angeles or sandy tracts along the beaches that no one else could use for profitable purpose.* Years later airports were located in the deserts and aircraft factories in the hills of Inglewood for the same reasons: because land there was cheap. As for the oil fields menaced by the proximity of the Japanese, they were discovered and exploited *after* the Japanese had performed the horticultural miracles that enabled them to grow vegetables for the Los Angeles markets in what previously had been wasteland.

In short, the Issei and Nisei settlement of California in the 1920s and '30s had followed lines of economic rather than military force. And the oil and aircraft industries had followed, not led the way for the Japanese.

Warren's testimony before the Tolan Committee was even more alarmist on another aspect of the situation. The fact that not a single act of sabotage had been reliably reported in the interval between December 7 and the day of the Tolan Committee's San Francisco hearing struck the attorney general as evidence of an attempt by the wily Japanese to lull the citizenry into "a false sense of security."

"The only reason we haven't had a disaster in California is that it is timed for a different date. . . . Our day of reckoning is bound to come. . . . And at the present time every police station in this state, every sheriff's office, every law enforcement agency can be flanked by aliens with weapons we know absolutely nothing about. Gentlemen, I say to you that if we expect local law enforcement officers to compete against a situation of that kind, it is just like putting a blindfold over a man's face and asking him to go out and fight someone that he cannot see. . . .

"I want to say that the consensus of opinion among the law enforcement officers of this state is that there is more potential danger among the group of Japanese who were born in this country than from the alien Japanese who were born in Japan!"

Kenny always reminded those who criticized Warren that "Walter Lippman was saying things about 'the sinister lack of sabotage on the West Coast' that were just as crazy as anything Warren said." But he made no apologia for the contrast between Warren's support of the "relocation" of Japanese-Americans and his vigorous opposition to a proposal, introduced in the legislature at this time, to prevent all enemy aliens from holding civil service positions. Warren argued that "naturalized

---

* AFTER 1913, Japanese were not allowed to buy any land in California.

citizens and their descendants have in the past and do now represent the highest standards of American citizenship. . . . To question their loyalty or place them in a category different from other citizens is not only cruel in its effect upon them, but it is disruptive of the national unity which is so essential in these times." No legislation discriminating against German or Italian aliens or their descendants was enacted in California even at the height of the hysteria.

Kenny's tolerance of Warren's "unfinest hour" may have been partly due to his sense of having himself "failed to set any sterling example of interracial amity" in the state senate. "I didn't pour any gasoline on the fire in those first days, but I wasn't in there with a hose trying to put it out." (RWK)

The courage which so impressed Robert Powers was exhibited when Kenny was attorney general under Governor Warren at the time the Japanese were permitted to return from their exile. In December 1944, the U.S. Supreme Court held (in a case known as *ex parte Endo*) that there was no legal basis for holding the Japanese in the concentration camps into which they had been herded. The war was still going on. California (and other American) families were still losing sons in battles with the Japanese on Iwo Jima and Okinawa. And there was no doubt that there were going to be problems for those Japanese who exercised their right to return to their homes in California. (Many did not.)

"To show you how serious the situation was, I remember the Mayor of Los Angeles saying, 'Bob, I hear you're advocating the return of the Japanese. Is that so?' I said it wasn't a question of advocacy; there just wasn't any authority for excluding them. And he said, 'Well, if they do return, I won't be responsible for their safety in Los Angeles.' " (RWK)

Kenny had some advance warning of the Endo decision and did what he could to make preparations. For one thing, he passed along his advance notice to Governor Warren, who issued a statement saying that in the event of a decision invalidating the exclusion order, the state authorities would stand "for law and order and justice" for the returnees. Governor Warren's pronouncement was not calculated to impress law enforcement officers who could recall the passionate utterances of Attorney General Warren three years before.

As Robert Powers put it: "The message was not clear in Warren's statement. But Kenny called a special meeting of sheriffs and D.A.s from all over the state and made them listen to his statement of intentions. There was no misunderstanding Kenny when he said that his department intended to see to it that the returnees were not molested."

The next step Kenny took was an example of his "prophylactic"—i.e. preventive—approach to law enforcement. In June 1943 there had occurred in Los Angeles a series of riots against Mexican-Americans, and one of Kenny's first acts as attorney general was to head off any recurrence of such events by educating the local police department in "ways to pick up warning signals well in advance of any racial disturbance; ways to build better relationships between minority groups and the police; ways to stop the circulation of rumors and to reduce other types of tension."

The teaching instrument was a little pamphlet, known as the Blue Book, written by Carey McWilliams, which was distributed to all California police officers. "It was circulating in other states as well because they were having race riots in Harlem and in Detroit. Now, with the new strains imposed on California, we got out an updated edition and spread it around in those areas where professional patriots were beginning to erupt." (RWK)

The "eruptions" of the first half of 1945 were "shocking and absurd," but not particularly inflammatory. Local American Legion posts disgraced themselves by voting to remove the names of Nisei servicemen from their honor rolls, despite the magnificent war record of Nisei volunteers in both theatres of the war. There was vandalism against Japanese-owned property, including a Buddhist temple in San Francisco where some of the early returnees found temporary housing. In Placer County there were some scare shootings that might have caused casualties but in the end, did not. And the home of one family in a small town called Loomis was burned to the ground just before they were due to return to it.

"That time the vigilantes overreached themselves. The War Relocation people, who were supervising the return, let it be known that this particular family had four sons in the armed services, one of them already dead overseas, and three decorated for bravery. The town's conscience was touched. Money was collected, and one of the churches undertook to see to it that a new house was built.

"There's no question, however, that there was a real attempt, with organizational backing, to drive these people out of California. The motives were interesting. We conducted quite an investigation on that point in the area around Fresno, where we found that the anti-Japanese sentiment was generated for the most part by a village banker who had been a great friend of the Japanese when they were being evacuated. There had been no time for them to make arrangements, and what happened there must have been fairly typical. Our friendly banker said, 'I'll take care of your property for you while you're gone,' never expecting to see them come back. But now here they were(!) and probably getting set to ask for an accounting! We had pretty solid evidence against this worthy steward, but before we could proceed, he had a heart attack and died. If we had been able to develop the case, it might have gone a long way toward explaining the economic motives of patriotism in that corner of California." (RWK)

Kenny's frontal attack on the bigots came only after extensive flanking movements by what he called his "roving prophylaxis team." One or two men from his staff, including Special Deputy Charles Johnson, would turn up in a town where they had been warned by the War Relocation Board that there were going to be a number of returnees. The task force would drop in on a whole galaxy of local v.i.p.'s: the sheriff, the police chief, the mayor, the board of supervisors or city council, the editors of the newspapers, and the commanders of the American Legion and V.F.W. posts.

The prophylaxis team would offer these authorities and opinion makers "any help we can give you in seeing to it that the reception of the returning evacuees is going to be peaceful and orderly." The impression was conveyed that "big brother would be watching from Sacramento to see how things went."

Things usually went very well. There were only two cases where local authorities defied the prophylaxis team and the attorney general, who always made the "follow-up call." One of these instances of outright defiance was the sheriff of Nevada County.* He told Kenny, when he called, that the Japanese had no business coming back, were not entitled to any protection, and were not going to get any from the sheriff's office. When all efforts to cool the fires in Nevada County failed, Kenny asked Warren to call out the state guard.

---

* "THIS MAN," said Kenny, "had actually gone as far as to try to prevent the Southern Pacific Railroad from using Japanese section-hands on their right-of-way through his county!"

"But Warren wasn't as impetuous as I. He said why didn't I let him call the sheriff first. He did. I don't know what he said, but I know what I would have said in Warren's place: something like, 'Look here, this crazy Kenny is on my neck, and I'm going to have to call out the Guard unless . . .' " (RWK)

Warren also talked by phone to the sheriff of Orange County, who was taking the position "that it was unreasonable to ask him to get himself in wrong politically by defending the Constitution in the matter of these particular citizens."

The only two sheriffs defeated for re-election in 1946 were the sheriffs of Nevada and Orange Counties. Kenny was willing to concede that, "There may have been other factors involved— such as the strength of their opposition. But it's an interesting historical coincidence in any case." (RWK)

Another element in the prophylactic approach to racial amity was the posting of a reward. Kenny persuaded a wealthy San Franciscan to offer $5,000 for information leading to the arrest and conviction of any person causing—or even threatening to cause—physical harm to a returning Japanese. "I've always believed that since the people you're after in these cases are rats, the best way to proceed against them is to offer an inducement to their fellow rats to turn them in. We only had to pay the reward once, but the point is not the payment. Just the reverse. The object of prophylaxis is to prevent—to deter a significant percentage of incipient criminal behavior by serving notice that there is going to be a strong temptation to peach on anyone who indulges in it." (RWK)

Anti-Japanese feeling relaxed after V-J Day, but other equally explosive antagonisms were building between blacks and whites, particularly in the vicinity of the shipyards of the Bay Area, where the population had tripled in the years of the war boom, and unemployment was rising as war orders slacked off.

Kenny was, of course, not the only public servant concerned about forestalling the kind of race riots that had erupted in the U.S. after World War I. The American Council on Race Relations announced a conference to be held in Chicago to discuss ways of averting racial strife by building better relations between policemen and blacks. Kenny sent as his representative to this gathering, Robert Powers. It was an inspired choice.

"Powers was what the French call a 'white black-bird'—meaning a non-formally-educated intellectual. He'd been police chief of Bakersfield before he came on to Warren's staff, from which

I inherited him. I figured he could contribute something pretty special to that conference and probably get a lot out of it too." (RWK)

Powers listened for a while to the professors ("some of them black! which was a new experience for me") who were doing most of the talking, and he decided they didn't know anything about policemen. So he jumped in. "I told them that the stupid general remarks they were making were just as offensive to the police officers, like Chief Prendergast of Chicago, who was sitting there suffering in silence, as the worst of the words cops use in private about minorities and professors. I deliberately offended them."

To the police officers' surprise, the professors listened, nodded, and asked questions that led to more plain talk from Powers. "They were intellectually honest! They were there to learn as well as teach. They were ignorant in certain areas, but so were we. And I, at least, didn't mind being taught. It turned into what's now called an encounter group—sociologist vs. cop!"

From Powers's report on the Chicago experience, Kenny conceived the notion of setting up encounter groups (or "sensitivity training seminars") in areas of potential racial violence. One such area was the city of Richmond across the bay from San Francisco. Thousands of black workers from the South had settled in the vicinity of the Kaiser shipyards during the boom years. The closing of the yards was creating mass unemployment. The stage seemed to be set for the classic black-white post-war confrontation.

Kenny talked with the Richmond city manager and persuaded him to experiment with a pilot project involving fifteen selected policemen, who were to take a course of ten sessions under Powers's leadership. Considerable attention was given to the choice of representatives of various minority groups with whom relations were—or might soon become—strained. "For instance, we got hold of Walter Gordon who was—or had been until very recently—what was then a real rarity: a black policeman. He had also been an All-American football player, and was later a federal judge in the Virgin Islands. We had Joe Grant Masaoka from the local Japanese-American Citizens League. (Joe was one of those incredible Masaoka brothers who collected an average of over five medals per man for bravery of one kind or another.) There was another Nisei, Staff Sergeant Ken Kato, who had just returned from service with the marines at Guadalcanal and Leyte. And there was E.W. Lester, former deputy police chief of Los Angeles. Someone asked Powers what minority Lester represented, and Powers said, 'The police.'

"That was the genius of his approach: he drew the parallel between the stereotyped thinking about blacks and Jews and Japanese, and the stereotyping of cops. He talked about the popular image of the policeman as an ignorant, brutal, flat-footed fellow who could be outwitted by any private detective and most laymen. And those Richmond cops dug it! They saw the parallel between words like 'nigger' and 'kike' and 'Jap', and so forth, and 'flat-foot.'

"The sessions were all set up on more or less the same basis: anything went, and there was some very frank questioning by both sides. For example, one of the policemen asked why so many of the internees up at Tule Lake had elected to renounce their American citizenship and accept deportation to Japan. That gave Joe Grant Masaoka a chance to tell the story of the evacuation from a viewpoint some of these people had never considered: the loss of everything a whole generation of hard-working men and women had managed to acquire; the loss of dignity; the separation of families—like the one that was forced to move on while the mother was on her death bed!

"The fact was, Joe Grant Masaoka's mother was confined in that hell-hole up in the Owens Valley all the time her sons were fighting and dying for the country that put her behind barbed wire!" (RWK)

To Kenny the proof of this prophylactic pudding was what happened—or rather, what failed to happen—in Richmond within a month of the seminars. Just the sort of triggering incident the city manager had been dreading occurred at one of the schools. There was a fight on the playground; one of the combatants got a bad cut on his leg; rumors began to circulate to the effect that it had been amputated. "And pretty soon, they were saying he was dead. There was a real gang-buster of a race riot in the making! But our enlightened cops went in and cooled it. It never got off the ground!" (RWK)

The substance of the Richmond seminar was incorporated in a booklet entitled *A Guide of Race Relations for Police Officers* and sent to all the officials who had received the little "Blue Book." The American Council on Race Relations was so favorably impressed that it paid for a second printing and circulated it all over the country, wherever it was anticipated that racial friction might get out of hand.

7.

The Gaffe

KENNY COULD HAVE BEEN ATTORNEY GENERAL FOR the rest of his life," according to Justice Raymond Peters. "Or he could have waited four more years to run for governor and come in at a walk. Instead of that, he decided to run against Warren in 1946. That, in my opinion, was the greatest single political calamity the state of California ever suffered."

That estimate is based on Peters' belief that Kenny was the best attorney general the state ever had and that Kenny's decision to run "in the wrong year" cut short his political career.

Of that decision Kenny himself said that "it looks pretty stupid in retrospect. But we know a lot of things we didn't know when I made it.

"Remember that we had a united Democratic Party at the end of 1944. We had won every possible election contest and some that weren't considered possible. The Republicans were so terrified they were ready for any sort of social compromise. (Earl Warren came out for that great 'socialist' doctrine of health insurance!) We Democrats thought we owned the world.

"Of course some things had happened between that 1944 high water mark and January 1946 when I had to make up my mind about running. The war had come to an end for one thing, and Roosevelt had died. At the time those events didn't seem likely to change the whole course of history. We know now that they did.

"As far as history was concerned, we could all have turned in our suits and headed for the showers the day Roosevelt was replaced by an ignorant, malevolent border politician, who set out to reverse all Roosevelt's policies on cooperation and coexistence with the Soviet Union, not to speak of his domestic programs. People forget that it was Truman who threatened to draft striking railroad workers into the army and instituted the infamous Loyalty Oath for federal employees. He was just filled with prejudices—against black and other colored minorities and most of all against 'reds.'

"But we didn't know all this at the end of 1945. We were dazzled by the colors of what turned out to be our sunset. And it was a glorious one! That California Emergency Legislative Conference, for instance. It's hard to believe even now that it was our last stand." (RWK)

The California Emergency Legislative Conference of January 1946 was the last and most impressive act of Kenny's tenure as attorney general, and a preview of his candidacy for governor. The notion of a grass roots, ad hoc, consultative assembly on the legislative needs of a state converting from a war to a peace-time economy had originated in the left-labor wing of the Democratic coalition that intended to enter the 1946 elections with Kenny at the top of their ticket. But so wide was the appeal of the proposal that the call that went out was signed by Kenny and a Republican co-chairman, Bartley Crum of San Francisco.

Sponsors of the conference included officials of the state C.I.O.; professors from Berkeley and Stanford; Hollywood personalities; California's authentic war hero, Col. Evans Carlson of the U.S. Marines; a black insurance company executive; a black judge from Los Angeles; officers of the League of Women Voters; department store tycoons; social workers; and farm leaders.

The day-to-day work of organizing was assigned to recruits from the ranks of trade unions and other groups of interested citizens, including, no doubt, branches of the Communist Party. Directing their effort was a staff of organizers, including a deputy attorney general, assigned full time to the recruitment of delegates. Cars from the attorney general's stable of vehicles (confiscated from traffickers in narcotics, etc.) were at the disposal of those who had errands to run. The facilities of the attorney general's three offices—one in Los Angeles, one in San Francisco, and one in Sacramento—were also made available. Phones, desk space, mimeograph machines, ink, and paper were there—free—to be used.

The response to the call and the recruitment campaign all but overwhelmed the organizers. Twelve hundred people descended on Sacramento—700 of them delegates, the rest, observers. One of the unpaid workers who sweated out the resultant crisis described it as a "no room at the inn situation."

"There had been no preparation for accommodating numbers like that. The proceedings might never have got under way, what with people milling about trying to make sure they'd have a place to sleep. But fortunately there was one woman from Los Angeles who was a sort of genius at emergency organizing. She took over.

"Somehow she collected a staff of telephoners and turned them loose on the Sacramento phone book. Some way, before that first day was over, she had a bed for everyone. It was crazy! And it was wonderful!"

The working sessions of the conference were conducted in several panel groups, in each of which definite, legislative proposals were hammered out.

The panel on housing, chaired by Langdon Post, of the Regional Housing Authority, recommended the outlawing of the racial restrictive covenant (which had not yet come before the U.S. Supreme Court). There was an Urban-Rural Relations panel, chaired by the Master of the State Grange. There were panels on child care legislation, equal job opportunity, veterans' affairs, full employment, social security—all the issues facing the people of the state.

It was widely understood that the program made up of these legislative proposals was the platform on which Kenny and other Democrats were going to run in 1946. Kenny made the major address, and the continuations committee that was set up was expected, in due time, to turn itself into a Kenny Campaign Committee.

"The hitch in all this," according to one of the full-time organizers of the conference, who prefers to remain anonymous, "was that the coalition that was supposed to support this sort of a campaign was already falling apart. The Right, which had never been very comfortable in there, was getting ready to pull out and start on the war they'd wanted to fight from the beginning: the war against Russia, with Truman as their leader. And the Left was split. Even the Communists were choosing up sides, deciding whether to go with Earl Browder, who was about to be thrown out of the party, or with Foster , who was about to take it over. Looking back you see that it was like the end of a pendulum swing, the instant when it hangs there, changing direction. All sorts of crazy things can happen at a time like that, and this was one of them. Some of us should have known it, but I don't remember anyone who did."

Actually, by the time the Legislative Conference ended, there were a number of people who suspected that the omens were bad, among them Kenny himself. But he had no valid excuse for backing away from the expected announcement of his candidacy.

As the anonymous observer quoted above puts it: "He'd begun laying his plans a year before, putting out feelers, letting it be known that he was agreeable to a movement to draft him. He thought—we all thought!—there was going to be a big postwar depression for which the Republicans would be held responsible. Also, there's a political legend to the effect that the voters always want to switch parties at the end of a war. In California that would have meant putting a Democrat in the governor's chair, and nationally it would have meant a Republican in the presidency. A lot of people were predicting that Warren was going to make a try for that spot in 1948.

"The trouble was the expected depression was not showing up, and the legend about switching parties at war's end was going the way of a lot of such legends. But the boys who felt Kenny had made a commitment—and maybe he had—didn't see that. They weren't as smart as he was. They thought they could win anyway. Or maybe they didn't care. Or maybe it was some of both."

Labor—particularly its left wing, organized into the C.I.O. and led by Harry Bridges—had entered politics as never before during the Roosevelt era. Political action committees were combat-ready and waiting for their marching orders. It was a gubernatorial year; the banner had to be carried by a candidate for governor; and there was no one who could make that race with labor's backing but Robert Kenny.

Philip (Slim) Connelly, then head of the southern wing of the state C.I.O., remembers that "all the political pros were beginning to say that Warren was unbeatable, and nobody wanted to stick his neck out by running against him. But labor thought it knew more than the pros. We had some illusions in those days—and some hopes. You have to remember what everyone thought was going to become possible in the aftermath of the war to end fascism: a real people's government in the U.S., overturning all the old political forms. And there they were— all those hopes!—in the legislative proposals that came out of the conference. No one but Kenny could run on that platform. And not to run would have been to give up the fight without even trying. To let the Roosevelt coalition fall apart without putting up a fight! If Kenny had refused, he would have been kicking what looked like the common man's best hope right in the solar plexus!"

In addition to the pressure from the Left, there was pressure from the center of the Democratic Party, gentler, perhaps, but in the same direction. Rollin McNitt, then chairman of the Los Angeles County Democratic Central Committee, believed that it was he and his counterparts in the San Francisco area who "persuaded Bob to run because we had to have a candidate and we couldn't get anyone else as good. Bob didn't think he should do it. I think he knew it was hopeless. I knew it too, in the sense that I knew he couldn't beat Warren, but I thought he had a chance in the primaries."

Kenny wavered on the knife edge of decision all through January and early February. Opposition editors were beginning to predict that he would pull out and disappoint his "dissatisfied, disaffected, and decidedly suspicious coalition of left wingers, Communists, self-styled liberals, and Democratic regulars." The political columnist of the *Los Angeles Times* claimed to know that "in confidential discussions of Democratic leaders and C.I.O. political action groups, Kenny is being roundly denounced as a prima donna, a political opportunist, who thinks only of his own personal ambition. Many of the off-side remarks accompanying such conversations are not printable."

Some of Kenny's more conservative friends from his days in the state senate advised him not to run. Justice Philip Gibson recalled that when he was consulted, he "said it was a terrible mistake. I told Bob he was the Democratic Party's greatest hope for national office, and to run then would be sacrificing him. Bob said, 'Well, they're pressing me pretty hard in Washington.' I said, 'They should have it explained to them that they're wrong. If you want me to call them and tell them off, I'll do it.' And I did."

A few days later, Kenny, in his capacity as president of the National Lawyers Guild, received an invitation from Supreme Court Justice Robert Jackson to attend the Nuremberg War Crimes trial as one of the four representatives of the American Bar.* He accepted, and the U.P. wire service dispatch that carried the item also suggested that his decision to absent himself from the country at this time was Kenny's way of giving the

---

* NAZI PARTY OFFICIALS and German military officers were brought to trial on charges of having violated internationally accepted codes of war-time ethics and morality. Robert Jackson, U.S. Supreme Court justice who issued the invitation to Kenny, was one of the prosecutors.

Kenny campaigning at OPA rally, 1946.

Democratic Party in California an opportunity to select another candidate.

Instead, a few days before he was to leave for Germany, Kenny announced that he would be a candidate for the Democratic nomination for governor, on a ticket that included Jack Shelley, a state senator with a trade union constituency (later Mayor of San Francisco); Edmund G. (Pat) Brown, an obscure young district attorney (later Governor of California); actress Lucille Gleason, a political nonentity; and Will Rogers, Jr., and Ellis Patterson as rival candidates for nomination as U.S. Senator.

Even with the wisdom of hindsight Kenny always maintained that "given a united Democratic Party and control of the campaign, I could have beaten Warren in the primaries. We would have gone down to defeat in November because that was a year when Democrats were wiped out everywhere. But it would not have been the debacle that it was.

"The trouble was I didn't have control of a party that wasn't unified. The time I should have caught on to that was when the so-called 'harmony forces' insisted I sit down with them to make up a slate of candidates before I left for Nuremberg. The meeting was held in my office in San Francisco at the end of February, and except for my bright notion of nominating Pat Brown to run for my old job, the thing was a political disaster. We failed to realize that a harmony slate had become impossible. The coalition that looked so powerful at the CELC just a month before was already showing bad cracks.

"The problem came into focus over the question of a candidate to run for the U.S. Senate. For a while I thought we had a solution in the person of Col. Evans Carlson of Carlson's Raiders. He was revered by the Left, and the Right was awed by his political mystique. But Carlson was a dying man, and by January he knew it and withdrew his name.

"My next happy inspiration was James Roosevelt, who had served under Carlson. But he declined to run. And at this point the Left proposed Rep. Ellis Patterson, who had bolted the Roosevelt slate in 1940* and was therefore anathema to the regulars. He was certainly not going to fit into any 'harmony slate.'

"My last move was to suggest the name of Will Rogers, Jr. He had surrendered his seat in Congress to Patterson and gone off to war. He was returning at this time with a fine record, and I was naive enough to believe that Pat would consider himself obligated. I therefore invited Will to lunch and persuaded him to submit his name. The leak in this wonderful arrangement was that Patterson refused to yield. I should have remembered that in politics gratitude is defined as a keen sense of favors to come.

"When the harmony slate caucus met in my office that February evening and I couldn't persuade the representative of either Patterson or Rogers to withdraw, I made a fatal political blunder. Anyone who retained his normal sagacity would have

---

* PATTERSON, WHO WAS THEN lieutenant governor, ran his own slate in that election in an effort to gain control of the California delegation to the Democratic National Convention, and failed.

recognized that if party discipline was insufficient to enforce a decision on the senatorial slot, there should not be any slate at all. But I had been carried away by that blind optimism that afflicts candidates for public office. Also, I had led a charmed political life up to that point, and I was suffering from the delusion that the charm was implanted in my character and not removable by circumstances or surgery."

Kenny described the harmony slate with rival senatorial candidates as a "package deal with an option"—a phrase he had picked up from some old vaudevillians. Confident that he had "swept the Patterson-Rogers thing under the rug" and predicting that "we will all be able to campaign together joyously and hopefully," he turned his back on the impasse and went off to Nuremberg to observe the historic trials.

The campaign that followed was neither hopeful nor joyous. The late C.B. Baldwin* described it as one of the oddest that ever occurred in this country, "because the essence of American electoral politics is that you attack your opponent, and Bob just wouldn't attack Warren. Partly, I guess, because he knew him better than the rest of us did."

It was also because Warren had done what many political observers had predicted he would do: i.e., he absorbed enough of Kenny's liberalism to defuse most of the potential issues between them.

Warren's comment on the campaign, made twenty years later, was that he "never understood why Mr. Kenny chose to make the race. There had never been a cross word between us, but suddenly he made the decision, and of course it was his right. . . . He conducted a very restrained campaign. There was actually nothing in it to which I could take exception."

The resultant disaster at the polls was analyzed by Carey McWilliams in *The Nation* of June 1946 as "a struggle for control of the liberal movement in California. . . . The left wing seized upon the Patterson-Rogers fight as a means of pointing up a need for independent action and of sharpening the third party question. . . . The right-wing supporters of Rogers made things worse by launching an ill-advised attack on Mr. Patterson. At the center of the campaign where the major strength should

* AT THE TIME BALDWIN was one of the national functionaries of the National Citizens Political Action Committee (NCPAC); later he was the manager of Henry Wallace's 1948 campaign. He died in 1975.

have been concentrated a vacuum was created, and Mr. Warren proceeded, almost without a campaign, to fill it. . . .

"Liberals everywhere," McWilliams warned in conclusion, "would do well to ponder carefully the results of the California election . . . before they become committed to a final break with that peculiar coalition we call the Democratic Party. The man who can still prevent this breach from becoming irreparable in California is Bob Kenny. Despite his defeat, the soundness and wisdom of his leadership have been demonstrated."

McWilliams was not the only journalist who refused to give up on Kenny. John Gunther, in the original edition of his *Inside U.S.A.,* called him "something of a white hope for the West" and predicted a continuing career in liberal politics despite the defeat. (In later editions of the work the section on Kenny was dropped from the "Bouquet of Californians.") *Coronet Magazine* had a flattering article in type at primary time and had to do some fast galley corrections to back out of the prophecy that "California's vigorous Attorney General [who] hasn't lost a round in his fight for human rights . . . will be the state's next and youngest governor, and is likely to sit in the White House some day." By inserting the word "not" in the first verb, the writer brought his enthusiasm in line with late developments, but like Gunther and McWilliams, Dean Jennings still saw a brilliant future for Kenny in electoral politics.

But Kenny, who had never lost an election before this, never won another—until he ran for re-election to the Superior Court in 1968.

"The minute I was defeated in the primaries, the organization Democrats wouldn't have anything to do with me. . . . Both the national and the state committees simultaneously reached the conclusion that I was beaten because I was 'tainted with red support.' . . . One of the things that had made me valuable to the organization Democrats was that I was supposed to be able to control labor and the Left. Well, I had now demonstrated my inability to do that in connection with the Patterson thing. So in July, the Democrats held their state convention and decided to plump for Truman and dump the Left.

"James Roosevelt led the apostasy, and it was shocking to some of us who thought we were in a tradition founded by his father and dedicated to achieving a decent and durable peace. When James led the parade away from co-existence and toward Cold War, there were some people who took it as a sign from Sinai. 'What's good enough for F.D.R.'s son is good enough for us,' they said and rolled over with him.

"That was the tragedy of the 1946 debacle. The split inside the Democratic Party in California might never have occurred except for that. Jimmy Roosevelt might still have become state chairman, but he would not have been in control of the party machinery. I would have. Even a lame duck stays in control for two years. So the Democratic organization in the second largest state would have either been neutral on the Truman Cold War foreign policy or against it. And there would have been every chance of dumping Truman at the 1948 convention. Which would have given us a whole new ball game."(RWK)

Kenny never forgave James Roosevelt for this "apostasy." Two decades after Roosevelt took over the reins of the Democratic Party in California, Kenny still summed up his character in the (for him unusually bitter) phrase: "the truth is not in him."

But Kenny wasted no more time on local in-fighting. Less than a week after Truman's November victory, he left California to attend two meetings, one in Washington, the other in Chicago, "to rally the old New Dealers to discuss how to pick up the pieces after the defeats of 1946."

8.
The Debacle

TRUMAN DIDN'T KNOW MUCH ABOUT THE AGREEMENTS Roosevelt made with Churchill and Stalin because Roosevelt didn't bother to inform him. It all comes out in the memoirs—Stimson's, Eisenhower's, even Truman's.

"There was that terribly revealing thing that happened to Molotov right after Roosevelt's death. The Russians had decided not to send Molotov to the opening ceremonies of the United Nations, but we begged them to. So, out of respect for F.D.R., they did.

"Molotov came through Washington on his way to San Francisco and paid a courtesy call on our new President, and Truman started lashing out at him about the Yalta agreements. Truman didn't even know what the Yalta agreements said! He had his information from somebody who didn't know either or who deliberately deceived him and pumped him full of the London Poles' version of everything.

"Molotov said later he'd never been treated that way anywhere in his life. The Cold War started that day." (RWK)

The Yalta agreements, to which Kenny referred, were the result of a conference held as the war was coming to an end, in an effort to resolve the foreseeable problems of post-war "power zones." Churchill and Stalin had had a private meeting in Moscow before Roosevelt joined them at Yalta. The agreement reached between them (to which Roosevelt was not a party but of which he was informed) assigned to the British a "predominant influence" in Greece and a strong, but not dominant influence in Bulgaria. The Russians were to have a predominant influence in the Axis-allied countries lying along their borders, particularly Poland and Hungary.

When British troops wiped out Communist-led Greek resistance fighters, Stalin held to the bargain he had made and did not intervene, despite strong pressure from the international Left. But when hegemony in post-war Poland was awarded by the Russians to the Polish government-in-exile based in Lublin, the anti-Russian Poles in London (and American-Polish communities here) were outraged. Truman took up the cudgels on their behalf and spoke out in most undiplomatic language about Russian perfidy and broken promises.

The truth appears to be that he was entirely wrong about who had promised what. Roosevelt had accepted the Churchill–Stalin accord because he recognized Russia's need for peace on her war-ravaged frontiers. (And also, perhaps, because with the biggest army in the world already in position, the Russians could have forced the same terms if they had not been reached by negotiation.)

Unfortunately the new American President had not been a party to these negotiations, and those who advised him on foreign policy in the first days of his sudden assumption of leadership were men like Averill Harriman and Admiral Leahy—men who were almost fanatically anti-Soviet even at the time of the closest rapprochement between the war-time partners. Truman shared their bias. (He had stated his own view of sound American foreign policy in the first days of the war: that we ought to help whichever of the original combatants—Germany and the USSR—was losing, to assure their mutual destruction.)

During this period Churchill was out of power in England and free to express his personal feeling toward the Soviets—a hostility as implacable as Truman's. It was natural, under these circumstances, for Truman to invite him and for Churchill to consent to speak in March 1946 at a small college in a small city in Missouri, and to lay there at Fulton the ideological foundation for Truman's new foreign policy in the phrase that became its soubriquet, "The Cold War." (By 1950 Churchill was back in power and unable to indulge such impulses toward self-expression. He and Eden were eager for summit conferences and all other measures that might cool off what he himself had heated up. Only Truman remained adamantly and adventurously provocative.)*

* IN THIS CONNECTION it is not so hard to understand why Kenny once tried to cross-file Eisenhower's name in a Democratic presidential primary. "If we have to have a military man," he said at the time, "it's better to have a general of the army than a captain of field artillery."

Kenny on the "Town Meeting of the Air" radio program, 1947.

Whether Stalin's paranoia was triggered or merely reinforced by the American "betrayal" of the Yalta accords is one of the mysteries of the period that may never be resolved. In Kenny's view, the Russians were remarkably patient with Truman in the first two years of his presidency because they had no choice. But, also in his view, they made a serious mistake when they refused to take part in the Marshall Plan.*

"The Marshall Plan was designed to include them. It might have turned out—if they had accepted—that they wouldn't have got the money. But I was on the air a lot during that per-

* THE MARSHALL PLAN (European Recovery Program), announced on March 6, 1947, was intended to foster the post-war economic recovery of certain countries—mainly England, France, Germany, and Italy—by providing funds for industries, etc. The Soviet Union and its allies accused the U.S. of intervening in the recipient countries in order to dominate the European economy. The socialist nations did not apply for or receive such aid.

iod—on the Town Meeting and [radio] programs like that—and I was always getting hit over the head with 'those dirty Russians who weren't willing to take the money we weren't going to give them anyway.'

"All the Russians had to do was say, 'Fine! Thanks!' Because that's what they had wanted a few years earlier. The big promise Roosevelt made to Stalin at Yalta was, in effect, that if they needed money to rebuild their country, they could have it. But Truman comes in, and he's not President a month before he cuts off Lend-Lease without a word to anyone! He restores it for a while and then cuts if off again. So the Russians get even by turning down what he's probably not going to come across with anyway!" (RWK)

Henry Agard Wallace had been vice president during Roosevelt's third administration. When Truman won the nomination for that office at the 1944 convention, Roosevelt kept Wallace in the cabinet as Secretary of Commerce, a place he continued to hold in the Truman cabinet. Serving under the man who had, in a very real sense, "robbed him of his robe of honor," Wallace became increasingly uncomfortable in the face of what he considered dangerous deviations from the Roosevelt policy of peaceful co-existence with our war-time ally, the Soviet Union. On September 12, 1946, at a large meeting in Madison Square Garden he made public his criticism of the new bipartisan consensus on getting tough with Russia. Ten days later Truman fired Wallace from the cabinet.

The lines were drawn, but not in a simple "front" between Truman Democrats and those who still clung to Roosevelt's program. One group of the latter, composed of non- or anti-Communist liberals, formed what became known as Americans for Democratic Action. (This group contained Hubert Humphrey, Franklin D. Roosevelt, Jr., Sidney Hook,* Morris Ernst, and members of Congress like California's Chet Hollifield and Jerry Voorhis, who had just lost his seat to Richard M. Nixon). Another group, consisting mainly of members of the two organizations that had sponsored the September Madison Square Garden meeting,** decided to merge into a new organization called the Progressive Citizens of America. It elected as its national

---

* SIDNEY HOOK, professor of philosophy at N.Y.U.; an ex- and dedicated anti-Communist.
** THE INDEPENDENT Citizens Committee of the Arts, Sciences and Professions; and NCPAC (National Citizens Political Action Committee), whose base was the membership of the great industrial trade unions.

co-chairmen, the sculptor, Jo Davidson and Dr. Frank Kingdon.* Robert W. Kenny, who had hardly finished digesting the last of the ceremonial banquets that saw him out of office as attorney general, became one of its national vice chairmen.

"I was very happy," Kenny said, "to join with old friends and colleagues in an organization with the stated objectives of P.C.A., which I read very carefully. I also read the preamble to its constitution, but apparently the significance of some of its language escaped me. I agreed, for instance, that:

> *Our government has fallen to men whose world vision is caught within a new isolationism. They view the world not as a brotherhood of peoples, but as an economic pie to be divided among cartels.*

"I also agreed that:

> *The Republican Party has long since lost any possible claim as a liberal party. The Democratic Party has repeatedly served the progressive cause. Under the administration of Franklin D. Roosevelt, our nation made significant democratic advances and charted a program for peace and security, embodied in the Economic Bill of Rights and in the principle of international friendship and collaboration. The Democratic administration has now abandoned this program. The Democratic Party is notoriously tainted with jim-crow reaction and machine greed. It is not clear now whether this party will recover its progressive tradition or surrender to its own brand of ignorance and bigotry.*

"What I failed to absorb was contained in the next few sentences, which read:

> *If the Democratic Party woos privilege and betrays the people, it will die and deserve to die. We cannot therefore rule out the possibility of a new political party, whose fidelity to our goals can be relied upon. We, the people, will not wait forever—we will not wait long for the Democratic Party to make its choice.*

* DR. FRANK KINGDON was a Methodist minister; chairman of the War Production Board, and member of the War Manpower Commission and Civil Defense Board; author, journalist, and news analyst. In 1945 he wrote a biography of Henry Wallace, *An Uncommon Man, or Henry Wallace and 60 Million Jobs.*

Backer Kenny and candidate Wallace, 1947.

"Someone certainly meant what that said because within a year the P.C.A. had disappeared into the third party, a suicidal course which I constantly opposed.

"This was the position of a political purist, the kind of a progressive who would rather see a reactionary elected than a 'lukewarm liberal.' The trouble with that is that in the election of a reactionary the political pendulum sometimes swings so far to the right that it gets stuck. Then it takes a cataclysm to get it swinging again." (RWK)

During the early months of 1947, however, the Southern California chapter of P.C.A., under Kenny's chairmanship, was organizing a list of sponsors, recruiting membership, and sponsoring a series of large public meetings to air opposition to Truman's loyalty oath program for government employees and his proposal to give Greece and Turkey $400 million worth of military and economic aid.

At one Los Angeles meeting, speaking in the name of the organization, Kenny denounced the latter as "a bold attempt to bypass the organization we helped set up to deal with this sort of problem—the United Nations," warning that it would involve the American people in the sort of unilateral action we had been saying we deplored when indulged in by others. "What it actually comes down to," Kenny said, "is that we are trying to save the King of Greece from his own people."

In April 1947, P.C.A. brought Elliott Roosevelt, who had just returned from a tour of the Soviet Union, to Los Angeles, to address a mass meeting at the Shrine Auditorium. The affair was such a success that "we began to feel ourselves rising like surfers on a big one" (RWK), and the Southern California Executive Board decided to present Henry Wallace at the Hollywood Bowl on May 17th.

"None of us anticipated any problems about engaging the Bowl. It had been used by all sorts of controversial figures, from Charles Lindberg to Claude Pepper, so we just sent our application in and began getting out the publicity. But the Board of Directors of the Bowl rejected our application on grounds that 'The Association does not believe that cultural interests are served by making the Bowl a forum for the dissemination of propaganda, or a sounding board for controversial issues.' That was a sign that the earth was already shifting under our feet!" (RWK)

There was some discussion of instituting a "citizens' suit" against the Bowl's directors, but in the meantime, the P.C.A. hired Gilmore Stadium, an outdoor arena used mainly for sporting events.

"Relations between P.C.A. and the Democratic State Central Committee were still reasonably pleasant at this time," Kenny said. (Local Democratic clubs had been debating and for the most part dissenting from Truman's new domestic and foreign programs. Hundreds of grass roots political groups, and even the Los Angeles County Democratic Central Committee, had wired the President asking him to reconsider.) On the matter of the Bowl's refusal to permit the Wallace meeting, James Roosevelt, in his official capacity as state chairman, wrote Kenny expressing his regret that the facilities should have been refused "to any speaker presenting any political views, no matter what they may be," but calling attention to the fact that "this does not indicate the committee's approval or disapproval of such views."

The Gilmore Stadium drew an overflow crowd of more than 27,000 people. Kenny introduced the main speaker in one of those "the man who" speeches, at the climax of which he said, "I give you Henry Wallace, the man for 1948!"

The crowd rose to its feet and began to chant the phrase, over and over, like rooters at a college football game. "Wallace in '48!" The managers of the meeting finally had to blink the lights on the field to quiet the crowd so that Wallace could begin to speak in the radio time that had been purchased for him. Even so, he was faded off after about fifteen minutes, and the station that had carried him was flooded with calls protesting this "outrageous piece of censorship."

"Wallace's speech was a real rouser, with again one of those hints of enthusiasm for a third party that slipped by me. He said, 'If the Democratic Party betrays its tradition by refusing to give expression to the liberal will of the people, they, the people, will find expression in other ways.'

"Some of the state and county central committee people who attended an informal reception for Wallace before the meeting tried to smoke him out on the third party question. They reported having got a different formulation—though if you read it with the perspective of what happened, maybe it wasn't so different after all. What he told them was, 'If the Democratic Party departs from the ideals of Franklin D. Roosevelt, I shall desert altogether from that party.' Since we California Democrats didn't see ourselves doing that, I suppose we were simply tone deaf to the warning note." (RWK)

Wallace's triumphal progress up the coast included meetings in the San Francisco Opera House and on a Berkeley street corner. (He had been denied permission to speak to the students on campus.) Kenny made the introductions in both cases and felt that his pitch was enthusiastically received. "Like Wallace, I was carried away by all the cheering, so when I was invited to speak at a banquet given by my old college fraternity, Phi Gamma Delta (this was an annual event called the Pig Dinner, and had been instituted in the first place by Frank Norris when he was a student), I gave the brothers a discussion of the parallel between Norris, the novelist, and Wallace, the politician. My point was that Norris had introduced a whole new school of realism into American literature, and that Wallace was introducing a comparable vein of political realism, or nonconformism.

"I was hissed!—something I was not at the time inured to— and the suggestion was made that I go back to Russia. I told the brothers that I didn't have to do that and elaborated by telling the story of the congressman who protested against the thoughtlessness of a fellow passenger who kept passing through the smoking car and leaving the door open. The congressman finally asked the door-opener if he had been born in a barn, and the door-opener said, 'You can kiss my ass.'

" 'I don't have to, replied the congressman sadly. 'You don't live in my district.' " (RWK)

This was the period during which Truman and the Democratic National Committee were trying to whip all recalcitrant state committees into line on the proposal to aid Greece and Turkey. After the Los Angeles County Committee urged the President to reconsider, they were informed that Secretary of the Treasury Snyder would not be able to fulfill his commitment to speak at their Jackson Day dinner. Eventually, after the rebuff had time to sink in, Mrs. Roosevelt agreed to appear as a substitute attraction. Invitations were mailed out over the signature of her son, James. Kenny received one.

Tickets were priced at $100 a plate, but Kenny decided to pay up and attend, "to show that it was possible to disagree with Truman and still remain a Democrat." He arrived on the evening of June 5, spoke with the guest of honor, and went to look for his place, assuming he would be seated somewhere at the head table, "above or below the salt," in view of the fact that as recently as a year before this time he had been "the only Democrat in California with a foot in the door of state office." But he found no place card, and when he asked one of the arrangement committee members, he was told that no place had been set for him. He went home.

The newspapers noted his exit and called to ask him why he had walked out. He was quoted as saying that he had been "edged off the dais," which was, as the *Herald* editorial put it, "a funny way to get purged."

Irritated, but by no means discouraged, Kenny continued to assume leadership of the Wallace for President movement. When Jo Davidson's failing health forced him to resign as co-chairman, Kenny replaced him.* He toured the country making speeches, with and without Wallace, with and without the assistance of crowd-pullers from the entertainment industry. And in

* OTHERS ON THE P.C.A. executive board at this time included Dashiell Hammett, author of *The Thin Man* and other detective novels; Aubrey Williams, publisher of *The Southern Patriot,* a veteran New Dealer from Alabama; and A.J. Whitney, of the Railroad Brotherhoods.

July, he returned to California to attend a conference in Fresno which was to organize Democrats for Wallace.

"This was my baby. I tried to use it as a springboard for the struggle I believed to be essential—a struggle to reshape the Democratic Party—or rather, to return it to the shape it had been in when Roosevelt headed it." (RWK) There were 325 delegates from all over California, all supplied with buttons that said, "Wallace in '48." But Kenny did not consider that he—or the conference—was heading for a third party. In fact, he met that question head on in his address:

> *Are we starting a third party? The answer is no. . . . We are here as Democrats, fighting for a live and progressive Democratic Party . . . for the nomination of Henry Wallace as the presidential candidate of the Democratic Party . . . starting the machinery for a delegation that will be for Wallace all the way with no compromise.*
>
> *There was no third party talk in the days of F.D.R. because the Democratic Party, as the party of the people, held out hope to independent voters. . . . The Democratic Party is not the party of Rankin and Bilbo . . . or of Truman and the Missouri gang . . . not the property of any group or clique. The Democratic Party, numerically, ideologically, and historically, is by a vast majority, the party of liberal voters [and] can only be mobilized around a fighting liberal program. . . .*

As expected, the delegates adopted a plan to place a Wallace delegation on the ballot of the California presidential primary of 1948.

One week later, James Roosevelt called a special meeting of the Democratic State Central Committee. Many of the Fresno delegates attended, suspecting that there would be an effort to push through an endorsement of Truman's foreign policy. They were right. It came in the form of a resolution, which Kenny described as "endorsing our commitment to use the U.N. as the intervening agency in international disputes, but adding that if it suited our convenience, we would bypass it as we were already doing in Greece and Turkey."

Kenny led the resistance to the resolution, attempting to defeat it without destroying what unity still existed in the party. For a while it looked as if he had engineered a compromise that would leave both sides feeling they had gained a point or two. "But it backfired, due to one of those inescapable slipups that haunt the manipulators of space crafts as well as political movements." (RWK)

Through July and August, Kenny continued to work on Democrats for Wallace, trying not to look over his shoulder at the lengthening shadow of the third-party movers. On August 24th, 600 of them met in Los Angeles and formally launched the Independent Progressive Party of California, with Hugh Bryson, of the Marine Cooks and Stewards, C.I.O., as chairman. Kenny did not attend the meeting.

On September 5, James Roosevelt endorsed Truman as the Democratic candidate for President in 1948. The fight inside the California party was now out in the open, eight months before convention time. Both sides were girding loins and sharpening weapons.

Kenny went to Oregon and was convinced that Democrats there were willing and able to put Wallace's name on the ballot in their primary, which would precede the California election by about three weeks. By this time, he had accepted the existence of a third party movement and the necessity to work with it where possible. But he devoted all his energy and powers of persuasion to the attempt to convince Wallace and the P.C.A. leadership that it was suicidal to foreclose Democrats for Wallace "by initiating the quixotic attempt to obtain half a million signatures for a third party."* As late as the first week in December, Kenny was still trying. His last letter to the executive vice chairman of P.C.A. suggests that:

> *Mr. Wallace should announce that he will be a candidate for President and express the hope that he will be supported by the Democratic Party as well as by any independent groups already formed or which may be formed in the 1948 campaign.*
>
> *Immediately after this announcement, Mr. Wallace should telegraph leaders of the Democrats for Wallace movement in those states where they are now active, i.e., California and Oregon. Such wires should say that he appreciates their ef-*

---

* IN CALIFORNIA 275,940 valid signatures were required to put the I.P.P. on the ballot. In New York it was easier because there was a previously existing independent party (American Labor Party) under whose aegis Wallace's name could appear. Other state laws presented other, lesser obstacles. The California signature campaign did not get under way until January 1948, and Kenny said of it, "If they make it, it will be the most remarkable piece of political water-walking ever seen."

forts in his behalf and that he will make himself available personally to come to their states and speak during the presidential primary.

He received no answer.

On December 17, the P.C.A. Executive Board met in New York. Kenny was not present, but his co-chairman, Frank Kingdon, was. A vote was taken on a resolution to support the Independent Progressive Party, and it carried. Kingdon resigned. Kenny was "the only P.C.A. chairman left—the boy on the burning deck!" He did not resign. But he gave an interview that was printed in the *Los Angeles Daily News* the day after the New York P.C.A. meeting that said in part:

I am not tying up with the third party. I am not fighting it. I'm just not crawling into bed with it. I suspect that they will be back in the Democratic Party some day.

I am for Wallace, but I want him as the candidate of the Democratic Party. The progressives have taken the Democratic Party over before now, and they may again.

He walked softly in print and made even more desperate efforts to persuade Wallace and those around him to hold off any announcement that Wallace would choose to run on the I.P.P. rather than the Democratic ticket. "At one point I had backed up so far that I was pleading with him to let us put him on the ballot in the Democratic primary in Oregon and California whether he had already announced as an I.P.P. candidate or not. I couldn't even get him to say yes to that." (RWK)

On January 10, 1948, there was another convention of the P.C.A. in Chicago, and everybody opposed to the third party resigned—except Kenny. Jo Davidson was still ill and out of the country. Kingdon had already quit. A.J. Whitney and Henry Morgenthau had come out for Truman. Despite his opposition to the course on which the organization was clearly embarking, Kenny was elected to a stop-gap chairmanship, and he still did not resign. "It really didn't matter, because within a few months the organization had resigned from me. Chapter by chapter it dissolved itself and merged into the I.P.P. In California it took us until June 17, by which time Democrats for Wallace was mostly a state of mind with a small deficit." (RWK)

Kenny always believed that the defection of progressives in California from the struggle to make Wallace the Democratic candidate had the effect of turning the party over to the forces of reaction. The argument advanced by some apologists for the I.P.P.—that it forced Truman to adopt some of Wallace's platform—Kenny dismissed by amendment: "If not to adopt, at least to talk about it.

"The I.P.P. did get on the ballot, of course. I didn't think it could, and it has been suggested by some cynics that its success was due in part to some unsought cooperation from Republican clerks checking petition signatures. The final vote for Wallace was only about 170,000, whereas the number of signatures declared valid was 275,000 plus.

"But regardless of that, what we lost was the opportunity of reshaping the Democratic Party in the second biggest state in the Union. It had taken us many years of hard work to get a two-party system in California. But we had it under Roosevelt, and the progressives had control of the machinery of that second party. I don't say we could have nominated Wallace on the national ticket, but we might have been able to dump Truman at the convention and get some sort of compromise candidate. (Maybe Bill Douglas, whom I had wanted to nominate in 1944.) And when it was all over, we would have still had a viable progressive party in the state.

"Also, if everybody had fought Truman inside the Democratic Party, there would have been a real consequential fight against the Cold War. The only reason Truman was so successful with his bipartisan foreign policy—which went down fine with Vandenberg and Dulles—was that there was nobody in his own party to say him nay, nobody to frighten him. Because the people who opposed him had lept off into the Progressive Party, severed themselves so they couldn't have a voice in the Democratic Party." (RWK)

Kenny noted with some bitterness that there was really no Truman campaign in California in 1948. "No one could get up the stomach for it. If the Republicans had had the sense to turn their ticket about and run Warren for President and Dewey for Vice President, they would have carried California and maybe the country. And Warren would have made as fine a President as he later did a chief justice."* (RWK)

---

* KENNY WROTE a summary of his view of the I.P.P. and the Wallace campaign in a long letter to Professor Curtis MacDougall in connection with the latter's book, *Gideon's Army* (N.Y. Marzani & Munsell, 1965, 3 vols). The letter is reproduced as Appendix B of this work.

9.
The Unholy Ten

PROGRESSIVE DEMOCRATIC OFFICEHOLDERS HAD SOME hard choices to make in the aftermath of the Truman victory. One way to stay in business was to trim sail to the new wind. Confessing to "having been duped" by unidentified Communists within the Democratic Party's leadership was all that was required of most of the penitents. Others had to take an active part in the effort to purge from the ranks any still unidentified subversives. Several had to endure short periods of underemployment. But in the end, most of those who had held state office in the Roosevelt era found places in the Truman era. Some, like Pat Brown, rose to the top echelons.

Since Kenny was obviously not one of the Communists to be hunted down and since he had been the party's top vote-getter up to the time of his defeat by Warren, he could probably have made his peace with those who succeeded him in control of the party machinery if he had tried hard enough. He didn't try at all.

One member of the California Democratic Central Committee (of this time), who asked not to be identified by name, said that "If he had even taken to the storm cellar and sat it out quietly, they would have been glad to forgive and forget when the storm was over. Instead of that, Kenny just moved from one set of confrontations to another. First the Democrats for Wallace thing. Then the Unholy Ten."

"The Unholy Ten" was a revealing slip of the tongue. What the committeeman meant to say was the Hollywood Ten—the motion picture writers, directors, and producers whose defiance of the House UnAmerican Activities Committee's probe of "Communist infiltration of the motion picture industry" led to the institution of the blacklist that was to cripple the cultural life of the U.S. for years.

It began with the issuance of some forty-five subpoenas, requiring the recipients to appear in Washington, D.C., in October, 1947, to answer questions in a public hearing conducted by HUAC. Nineteen of the forty-five declared themselves publicly and well in advance to be unsympathetic to the purposes of the investigation. They retained the services of a half dozen attorneys, including Kenny, who was less than a year out of office as attorney general.

At this time Kenny was leading the anti-Truman struggle within the Democratic Party, and he came to believe that the Hollywood investigations were an outgrowth of that intramural struggle. In his view, "It may have all begun in that great Gilmore Stadium meeting where we kicked off the Wallace for President boom. One of the speakers on the platform that night was Katharine Hepburn, and she attacked the Motion Picture Alliance for the Preservation of American Ideals (that was a Hearst-sponsored pressure group in the industry that was always complaining about Communist influence in pictures like Sam Goldwyn's *The Best Years of Our Lives.* There was a long list of others they didn't like, most of them Academy Award winners, at least the ones that had followed the old Warner Brothers formula about 'combining good picture making with good citizenship,' . . . Or was it the other way around?). Anyway, this was one of the things Hepburn went after in that speech.

"It probably irked the Ideal Preservers. Also, she wore a very striking red dress, something that fluttered in the wind like a flag. A red flag! I'm sure that didn't go unnoticed. But the worst thing was the collection that was taken up to defray the expenses of promoting our candidate. You know how that sort of thing is done: whoever is at the microphone likes to announce the names of big givers. And there were contributions announced from motion picture luminaries and Cornelius Vanderbilt, Jr.—quite an array of fiscal responsibility! Actually, few people gave over $100, but the impression was created . . . Well, let's say that in the popular mind whatever was collected became exaggerated to an astronomical extent. And I'm sure that rang the panic button on the other side.

"The Ideal Preservers got busy and called on Mr. Thomas for help. That's J. Parnell Thomas, who was chairman of the House UnAmerican Committee. (Feeney, as some irreverent critics used to call him because that was his name before he climbed too high on the political ladder to carry such a burden.) Now, a year earlier there had been a drive in the Hearst press to get this committee out to Hollywood. But that was under the 79th Congress, which was Democratic-controlled. They didn't respond to the Ideal Preservers. Possibly they felt pressure from the motion picture producers, many of whom were big campaign contributors and who didn't want any of this sort of havoc wrought in their compounds.

"But the 80th Congress was different. There had been a big Republican landslide—the one that buried me—and Thomas, who was a Republican, had succeeded to the chairmanship of HUAC. And no one—not even the motion picture producers— could head him off.

"Thomas turned out to be something of a crook in regard to the way he ran his office. Eventually he ended up in the pokey for taking kickbacks from his staff—the same pokey and at the same time as a couple of the Ten, who were there for having displayed contempt for him! But you have to say this about Thomas: he was very serious indeed and not to be deflected from what he considered his duty when it came to investigating the subversives of Hollywood. He probably read the Hepburn speech, and it probably confirmed his worst fears." (RWK)

Kenny was out of California when the storm burst, on business connected with the P.C.A. "A good part of that summer and early fall I was touring the country, drumming up support for Wallace. We had a program put together by some political talent agency: there was a motion picture star, John Garfield; and a musician, Larry Adler; and a dancer, Paul Draper; and me. I was the pitch man. We played Denver and Salt Lake City with that combo, and then I played some dates without the top bananas. In October, I was in New York.

"Actually I wasn't there entirely on Wallace business. I was there for the Yankee-Dodgers World Series. I was at Ebbetts Field the day Yankee pitcher Bill Bevens had a no-hitter going with a one-run lead and two out in the ninth. A Dodger pinch hitter named Cookie Lavagetto boomed a double off the right field wall and scored two men to win the game. The Brooklyn fans walked out of the stadium in a stunned, low-mumbling delirium. . . .

"I went on to Philadelphia to attend a board meeting of the P.C.A., and a phone call from Los Angeles caught up with me.

Subpoenas were out all over town, and I was wanted back to discuss the legal aspects of the thing. I was glad I'd seen that game. It was the last relaxation I was to enjoy for many months." (RWK)

On October 15, 1947, Kenny made his first public appearance on behalf of his new clients. It was a meeting at the Shrine Auditorium in Los Angeles, and eighteen of the Unfriendly Nineteen* were on stage with him. They were:

ALVAH BESSIE, screen writer, novelist, and historian of the Spanish Civil War.

HERBERT BIBERMAN, screen writer, director, producer, and stage playwright.

BERTHOLD BRECHT, German anti-Nazi refugee, poet, playwright, and author of two original screen stories.

LESTER COLE, screen writer and playwright.

EDWARD DYMTRYK, screen director.

GORDON KAHN, screen writer.

HOWARD KOCH, screen writer.

RING LARDNER, JR., screen writer (Academy Award winner, 1942), member of Executive Board of Screen Writers' Guild.

JOHN HOWARD LAWSON, critic, playwright, screen writer, first president of Screen Writers' Guild.

ALBERT MALTZ, novelist, short story writer, screen writer, playwright, member of Authors Guild and Authors League of America Councils.

LEWIS MILESTONE, screen director (Academy Award winner, 1928, 1930).

SAMUEL ORNITZ, novelist and screen writer.

LARRY PARKS, screen actor.

IRVING PICHEL, screen actor and director.

ROBERT ROSSEN, screen director.

WALDO SALT, screen writer.

ADRIAN SCOTT, screen writer and producer.

DALTON TRUMBO, novelist, screen writer (Academy Award nominee, 1938), member of Executive Board of Screen Writers' Guild, founding editor of The Screen Writer *(official organ of S.W.G.), and accredited war correspondent, 1945. (See footnote, page 106.)*

Introducing his clients to the audience at the Shrine that evening, Kenny said:

* RICHARD COLLINS was not present.

*I have never counseled a group of men so learned, so coura-
geous, and so thoroughly understanding of what the case is
about. Americanism today is what the debates, the wars, the
elections, and the litigation of the past have brought us.
These men know a great deal about Americanism and the
struggles by which it was won. They know that it must be
fought for in the legislatures, as well as on the battlefields. . . .*

*I am one of several lawyers for these men. We have all ad-
vised them that the powers of Congress are less than the force
of the Bill of Rights. . . . We have advised that when questions go beyond the powers of the committee or into the im-
munities of witnesses, they need not answer. In short, we
have advised that the Constitution of Holmes, Brandeis, and
Cardozo is as powerful as ever and worthy of confidence by
all who respect it. . . .*

*It is my proud privilege to tell you that each and every
man we represent has individually determined he will not
yield at any point in upholding the constitutional rights of
the American people and of the industry of which they are
a part.*

Actually there was one exception to that unanimous decision
to resist, and it is of some historical interest. Berthold Brecht
was not an American citizen and was, at the time he received his
subpoena, already packed to return to his liberated homeland.
He did not claim the rights or privileges of U.S. citizenship, but
he identified himself publicly on the side of those who had
taken a stand against the "inquisition."

On October 16, the Unfriendly Nineteen and their lawyers
left Los Angeles on a chartered plane, which someone nicknamed the Flying Tumbril. They stopped on the way for some
public meetings and arrived in Washington on October 19th.
That day, which was a Sunday, their lawyers conferred privately
with lawyers retained by the Association of Motion Picture
Producers.

A number of members of the Association had also been subpoenaed: executives like Jack Warner, Louis B. Mayer, and Sam
Goldwyn. Two nationally known political figures had been retained as counsel to represent them and "defend the industry."
These were Eric Johnston, Chairman of the Association of Motion Picture Producers, and Paul McNutt, the former governor
of Indiana.

Conferring with McNutt and Johnston at the Shoreham Hotel that afternoon were Kenny, Bartley Crum of San Francisco (who had co-chaired the California Emergency Legislative Conference of 1946), Ben Margolis and Charles Katz of Los Angeles, Martin Popper and Sam Rosenwein of New York. According to Katz, Kenny was unquestionably chief counsel at the meeting. "It was he who set the tone of that whole first week in Washington. He was the only one of us whom Johnston and McNutt respected enough to listen to. So it was Bob who undertook to tell them our view of the matter: that for the good of the country, as well as the industry, they must resist the committee's pressure to start a blacklist."

The argument, which turned out to be prophetic, was that if these nineteen men were blacklisted, hundreds of other people would be intimidated, and the result would be censorship of the democratically oriented mass medium of motion pictures, without the necessity to pass a single piece of legislation to that effect. The lawyers for the Nineteen were sure they could win the constitutional question before the U.S. Supreme Court, but they knew that might take a long time, and they wanted to make sure the Nineteen were not thrown out of the industry while the case was appealed. "We had to have some assurance that the producers would stand firm," said Katz, "and that's what Bob Kenny was after in this meeting. He laid it out beautifully. First, he pointed out that the Hearst papers were calling openly for censorship, and that the Thomas committee was aiming at getting it with or without legislative action. Johnston said something to the effect that he and his clients were of the same opinion. It was very smooth, very cool.

"Then Bob moved into the nitty-gritty area. He referred to some press releases by Thomas which stated that the producers had already agreed to 'clean their own house' with some sort of self-imposed purge. Johnston jumped as if he'd been stung! He would never under any circumstances be a party to anything so unAmerican as a blacklist, he said, and he was particularly hurt that his old friend, Bart Crum, should have suspected him of such a thing. Bart Crum got all choked up and shook Eric's hand and said he'd known all along it wasn't so, and more of the same.

"Well, the way it was working out was just too good to be true! As a matter of fact, it wasn't true." (It was discovered later that Johnston had actually proposed a blacklist under the euphemism of a "self-policing policy," which the producers' association had turned down on the advice of another counsel, who told them it would amount to a conspiracy and would be illegal until and unless Congress outlawed the Communist Party.)

Katz remembered of that Shoreham meeting, "that Bob was very tactful, but he wanted to be absolutely clear. 'Then your clients are not going to blacklist these men?' he asked. 'Absolutely not,' said Johnston, and McNutt agreed. And by the way, McNutt stood firm on this point even when Johnston crumpled, as he later did.

" 'And may we report this to our clients?' Bob asked.

" 'You tell the boys not to worry,' Johnston said, 'There'll never be a blacklist in Hollywood. We're not going totalitarian to please this committee!' "

Johnston maintained that stance for the duration of this particular set of hearings (although he was later to lead the retreat). His opening statement before the committee was so powerful that it was printed by supporters of the resistance as a full-page paid advertisement in the *New York Times*. That may have had some effect on the rest of the press (except for the obdurate Hearst–Patterson–McCormick group). Certainly the behavior of the committee's chairman, J. Parnell Thomas, had an effect on the press. Coverage, both domestic and foreign, was more sympathetic to the resisters than any of them had dared to hope. One British newspaper called the first week of hearings "a nauseating spectacle." Others culled the testimony of friendly witnesses for the most outrageous specimens of reactionary nonsense and printed them unexpurgated and without comment.

There was, for example, Mrs. Lela Rogers, mother of screen star Ginger, who offered as a sample of Communist propaganda that her reluctant daughter had been required to speak before the camera: "Share and share alike; that's democracy." And there was Ayn Rand, a Russian-born writer, who had left the Soviet Union in 1926 and testified as "an expert on the distortions of films made in Hollywood during the war, dealing with the Red Army." "One of the stock propaganda tricks of the Communists," Ms. Rand told the committee members, "is to show these people smiling!"

Other friendly witnesses rattled off lists of names of people they believed to be Communists or Communist sympathizers, adducing as proof in one case "a certain smell" to their associations and opinions. There were accusations that would have been grounds for libel suits in other circumstances: e.g., that high officials in the Roosevelt administration had forced motion picture producers to produce, and actors to act in films that were Russian propaganda vehicles. There was one particularly exotic tale about a former Navy pilot who did a little magazine writing on the side having been trapped by a literary agent into betraying to the Russians secret information on supersonic planes.

When Charles Katz, who represented the literary agent, rose to ask the right to cross-examine the witness making this charge, Chairman Thomas called the police and had the attorney thrown bodily out of the hearing room.

Quentin Reynolds, who had covered the European political front during the rise of Hitler, filed a story that day in which he pointed out the parallel between procedures of HUAC and those of the Nazis' "people's courts," where no legal safeguards were granted the accused, and where—in effect—the accuser functioned as judge, jury, and executioner.

"This is something new to men like Katz, and Crum, and Kenny, who have been practicing in courtrooms all their lives," Reynolds wrote in the newspaper *PM*. "They are completely bewildered by it. It is something they never learned about in law schools. . . . [I]t shakes their legal souls."

It also shook the soul of ex-Governor McNutt, who was still representing the Motion Picture Producers' Association. On the third day of the hearings he made a statement to the press, which said in part: "I was shocked to see the violence done to the principle of free speech during the hearings this morning. . . . You don't need a law to impair the constitutional rights of free speech. It can be done by intimidation and coercion. That is the way of totalitarian regimes that we all hate."

But man's capacity to maintain a state of indignant astonishment is relatively short-lived. By the end of the first week, the indignation was subsiding into distaste; headlines were diminishing in size, and coverage was shrinking. Acting to avert the threat of oblivion, Chairman Thomas leaked his program for the second week well in advance. The Washington wire services carried this summary of coming attractions:

"Next week the Committee starts getting what Chairman J. Parnell Thomas (Rep. N.J.) has called 'the other side,' from some of the people whose names have been brought up. The plan is to ask one man after another whether he is a Communist or ever was; then, depending on the answer, bring out any definite evidence the Committee has dug up. (All through the first week witnesses named people they had heard or believed or were sure were Communists or followers of the Communist Party line. But they had no proof.)

"A witness who refuses to answer could be cited for contempt of the Committee and of Congress.

"If a witness says he is not a Communist and the Committee thinks it has proof he is, it can ask the Justice Department to file a perjury suit. That also could result in a fine and jail sentence. If anyone admits he is a Communist, there is nothing the Committee can do beyond advertising it—there is no law against being a red. But the pressure then would be on his Hollywood boss to decide whether he should stay on the payroll."

At the opening session of the second week, Kenny and Crum were the first people heard. They moved that the committee dissolve itself for the reason that it was out of its constitutional bounds, if not fundamentally unconstitutional by its very nature. Their motion was denied.

Next Crum requested permission to recall for cross-examination a list of the first week "friendlies" who had attacked the characters and endangered the career of his clients. Chairman Thomas not only denied this request, but pounded his gavel loudly through the list of names and the lawyer's explanation, which was "in order that we may show that these witnesses lied under oath."

After that the first of the "unfriendlies" was called. John Howard Lawson brought to the stand a statement he intended to read into the record. Thomas gavelled his verdict on that "maneuver." Lawson protested that the friendly witnesses had been permitted to read long, prepared statements, some of which had attacked him personally. The gavel pounded louder, and Thomas threatened to have the witness removed from the stand. But the committee's counsel had not yet had a chance to ask the all-important, entrapping question:

"Are you or have you ever been a member of the Communist Party of the United States?"

Everyone leaned forward to hear Lawson's answer. If he said yes, he was going to be out of a job, even if the producers stood firm against blacklisting. For Lawson was not at the time under contract to any studio, and obviously no producer was going to hire any writer who admitted to Communist Party membership in the chill of an on-coming Cold War. If Lawson said no, he would certainly be faced with a prosecution for perjury, for a number of friendly witnesses had testified that he was considered to be "Mr. Communist" of the motion picture industry. If he refused to answer, he was going to be cited for contempt. Chairman Thomas had already said so and was now reminding the witness that four men who had been cited for similar non-co-operation had already served prison terms of six months to one year.

Lawson replied by attacking the right of the committee to ask such questions. The gavel pounded. Other members of the committee began speaking out of turn. The counsel, Robert Stripling, tried to regain control, but it was too late. The record shows the following exchange, although it reflects little of the background accompaniment:

CHAIRMAN THOMAS: (pounding his gavel) We are going to get the answer to that if we have to stay here a week. Are you a member of the Communist Party, or have you ever been a member of the Communist Party?

LAWSON: It is unfortunate and tragic that I have to teach this committee the basic principles of American———

CHAIRMAN THOMAS: (pounding the gavel) That is not the question. The question is: have you ever been a member of the Communist Party?

LAWSON: I am framing my answer in the only way in which any American citizen can frame his answer to a question which absolutely invades his rights.

CHAIRMAN THOMAS: Then you refuse to answer that question. Is that correct?

LAWSON: I have told you that I will offer my beliefs, my affiliations, and everything else to the American public, and they will know where I stand———

CHAIRMAN THOMAS: (pounding his gavel) Excuse the witness.

LAWSON: (continuing) as they do from what I have written.

CHAIRMAN THOMAS: (pounding the gavel) Stand away from the stand.

LAWSON: I have written Americanism for many years, which you are trying to destroy.

CHAIRMAN THOMAS: Officers, take this man from the stand!

The scene which followed was another "nauseating spectacle," for Lawson was lame and could not be hurried gracefully.

When order and decorum were finally restored, Stripling began to read into the record "one hundred exhibits showing Mr. Lawson's affiliation with the Party." These turned out to be a somewhat heterogeneous bill of particulars, including Lawson's authorship of a textbook on playwriting, a number of successful Broadway plays and Hollywood films, his espousal of the Fair Employment Practices Act, his opposition to the poll tax, his support of Franklin D. Roosevelt for a third and fourth term, and his opposition to the candidacy of Thomas E. Dewey—all mingled, indiscriminately, with the testimony of a roster of informers, some more, some less qualified to allege Communist Party membership.

Stripling read till his voice was tired and then turned the chore over to a subordinate. By this time the press and part of the audience had wandered into the corridor outside the hearing room, to debate the issue of whether or not Lawson had refused to answer the $64 question. Kenny was there, and reporters asked his opinion not only on what Lawson had actually done, but also on an even more troublesome question: why should anyone object to declaring his political affiliation in a free, democratic country?

"Possibly," Kenny replied, "for the same reasons we adopted the Australian ballot and have curtains hung over our voting booths." He explained that before the Australian ballot, Americans had to state their party affiliation to get a ballot in the general election, as they still must in a primary. He also called attention to the fact that General Dwight Eisenhower, then being touted as a possible candidate for the presidency, had refused to state whether he was a Democrat or a Republican.

The second witness called that day was Dalton Trumbo, who was said to be the most highly paid of the Unfriendly Nineteen. Like Lawson, he had brought with him a prepared statement, and, like Lawson, he was denied permission to read it. Before the $64 question was put to Trumbo, he was asked a $32 one: whether he was or had ever been a member of the Screen Writers' Guild.

Trumbo demanded the right to introduce testimony concerning his professional output and his personal character, and Stripling complained that the witness was not being responsive. Thomas's gavel began to pound again, and Trumbo was admonished to answer questions with a simple yes or no.

"I shall answer in my own words," Trumbo said. "Very many questions can be answered yes or no only by a moron or a slave."

He was ordered to stand down. Stripling read a dossier on Trumbo into the record, and another member of the committee's staff was called to the stand. A former F.B.I. man, Louis J. Russell, submitted in evidence a piece of stiff paper, which he identified as a Communist Party membership card, made out in the name of Dalt T. Russell testified that he had "obtained a code which reflects that the name, Dalt T., was used for Dalton Trumbo."

In the recess that followed the Russell disclosure, some of the newspapermen again sought out Bob Kenny, this time at the Washington Press Club, where he was a member. As a result of that conversation, Chairman Thomas read during his lunch a news item that said Kenny was advising his clients to refuse to state whether they were Communists.

The afternoon session began with the questioning of the third witness, Albert Maltz. But midway through the questioning, Thomas ordered the witness to stand down, and called Kenny. The record shows the following dialogue (which is used in law school textbooks in chapters on the privileges of the witness, as an example of the attorney-client privilege in action):

CHAIRMAN THOMAS: Mr. Kenny, the reason for calling you to the stand this afternoon is a newspaper article which appeared in this afternoon's Times-Herald.
MR. KENNY: Yes, I saw that too.
CHAIRMAN: I would just like to read it to you so that you are sure you know what I am referring to.
    "Counsel for 19 'defense witnesses' in the House Reds-in-filmland investigation said today he would advise all his clients to invite prosecution by refusing to say whether they are Communists. . . .
    "Hollywood attorney Robert W. Kenny said he would also advise the other 18 to walk the plank. . . ."
    Mr. Kenny, is that a correct quotation?
MR. KENNY: Well, Mr. Thomas, you put me in a doubly embarrassing position. As a former newpaperman, I have always made it a practice never to disavow anything that is ever printed in a newspaper. The other problem, of course, is the relationship between attorney and client and that is also a privileged situation. . . .

CHAIRMAN: *Did you advise your clients not to answer questions put to them by the committee or its chief investigator?*

MR. KENNY: *You are not a lawyer, Mr. Thomas, and, as I think your counsel, or someone, would advise you, that would be highly inappropriate. If there is one thing that is sacred in this country, it is the matter of advice that a counsel gives his clients.*

CHAIRMAN: *Oh, yes.*

MR. KENNY: *I am sure you didn't intend to invade that.*

CHAIRMAN: *I appreciate that. I am not a lawyer. I admit that.*

MR. KENNY: *No.*

CHAIRMAN: *But I would like to know, as the chairman of a congressional committee, whether or not you, as the attorney for these witnesses, advised them not to answer questions put to them by this congressional committee or its chief investigator.*

MR. KENNY: *Mr. Thomas, I would be disgraced before every one of the 100,000 lawyers in the United States if I answered that question. That is one thing that cannot be answered. . . .*

CHAIRMAN: *Have you got the statute there, Mr. Stripling? . . . I would like to read the statute because if you did give them that advice you would be doing everything you possibly could to frustrate this congressional committee, and you would be in more serious trouble than some of your witnesses.*

MR. KENNY: *Well, Mr. Thomas, I am not here to be lectured by this committee. . . . I do think that it is the highest impropriety to ask a lawyer what advice he gave his client.*

CHAIRMAN THOMAS: *I would like to read this statute: this is Criminal Code, section 37, Conspiring to Commit an Offense Against the United States. . . .*

"If two or more persons conspire either to commit any offense against the United States or to defraud the United States in any manner, or for any purpose, and one or more of such persons do any act to effect the object of the conspiracy, each of the parties to such conspiracy shall be fined not more than $10,000 or imprisoned not more than 2 years or both,"

Dated March 4, 1909

Now then, you say this Times *article is not a correct reporting?*

MR. KENNY: *Yes, Mr. Thomas, I had told you that I can-*

not, of course, tell you what advice I have given my clients. That is, without being dramatic about it, that would be an invasion of one of the most privileged communications that we have.

CHAIRMAN: No, no. I am asking you now about a statement you made to the newspaper, not a statement made to your clients. In what way has the article failed to report what you said?

MR. KENNY: This, as I say, puts me in the position of disavowing a newspaperman; but newspapermen aren't all lawyers . . . and I did not say that I would advise my clients to invite prosecution. That is the first paragraph.

CHAIRMAN: You didn't?

MR. KENNY: Because I think my clients have all behaved themselves in a manner that would not invite a successful prosecution. Now let's see the next paragraph: "Kenny said he would also advise the other 18 to walk the plank." I don't advise anybody to walk any plank. I am not that bad a lawyer.

CHAIRMAN: Well, I will tell you, Mr. Kenny, as chairman, I want to let you know that you squirmed out of this one temporarily, but if the committee should determine that there is a violation of this Conspiracy Act, then the committee will take under consideration referring the matter to the United States Attorney.

MR. KENNY: That is right, Mr. Thomas. I might say that the committee has squirmed out of one, too, because I am sure the committee did not intend to invade the sacred province of the relationship between attorney and client.

CHAIRMAN: Oh no, and neither would you want to commit conspiracy.

MR. KENNY: Neither one of us is intimidated, is that right, Mr. Chairman?

CHAIRMAN: We will have the next witness.

Before the witness was recalled, however, Kenny asked whether there would be an opportunity for counsel to "register a motion to strike from the record material in the dossiers of witness Maltz, witness Lawson, and witness Trumbo . . . on the ground that they are hearsay?"

Thomas replied that when all the witnesses had been called, and "we have got those dossiers, as you call them, well fixed into the record, we will be very pleased to have you make a mo-

tion." He added in a heavily casual parenthesis that he was not
sure how many more witnesses there would be since "I think
maybe you are losing a couple."

Things went more smoothly after this exchange. A pattern
was established: a witness would be called to the stand, denied
the privilege of making or reading a statement, and questioned
about Communist Party and Screen Writers' (or Directors')
Guild membership. Investigator Russell would produce a slip of
stiff paper which he alleged to be a Communist Party card with
a code name, e.g., Dalt T. or Ring L. Counsel Stripling would
read into the record an agglomeration of charges, and the next
victim would be called. By noon of the fourth day the only sus-
pense remaining concerned the identity of the witnesses whose
defection Thomas had predicted. Ten had been heard; nine remained; and again press coverage was sagging.

The last witness before the lunch break on that day was
a slight, unimpressive, mild-mannered man with a heavy German
accent, who was later to emerge as the most significant literary
talent of this talented ensemble. Both Stripling and Thomas
treated Berthold Brecht with patronizing politeness. They began by offering him the services of an interpreter. Brecht accepted, apparently catching them off guard. A hastily produced
consultant in philosophy for the Library of Congress turned out
to be less intelligible in English than Brecht, and in the end the
interpreter's services were not much used.

Kenny sat at Brecht's elbow through the questioning; both
men lit and smoked cigars. "Brecht brought the cigars, and gave
them to me before we went up. He told me that if I thought he
was getting excited to hand him one, and we'd light up." (RWK)

As usual (but with unusual courtesy) the committee denied
the witness's request to read a statement he had prepared, and
Stripling moved at once to the $64 question. For the first time
all week, he got a responsive answer.

"Mr. Chairman," said Brecht, "I have heard my colleagues
when they considered this question as not proper, but I am
a guest in this country and do not want to enter into any legal
arguments, so I will answer your question as fully and as well
I can. I was not a member or am not a member of any Communist Party."

*CHAIRMAN THOMAS: Your answer is, then, that you have
never been a member of the Communist Party?*
BRECHT: That is correct.

STRIPLING: You were not a member of the Communist Party in Germany?

BRECHT: No, I was not.

STRIPLING: Mr. Brecht, is it true that you have written a number of very revolutionary poems, plays, and other writings?

BRECHT: I have written a number of poems and songs and plays in the fight against Hitler, and, of course, was for the overthrow of the government.

CHAIRMAN THOMAS: Mr. Stripling, we are not interested in any works that he might have written advocating the overthrow of Germany, of the government there. . . .

STRIPLING: (reading) "Forward, we've not forgotten!/ We have a world to gain./ We shall free the world of shadow!/ every shop and every room;/ every road and every meadow!/ All the world shall be our own!" Did you write that, Mr. Brecht?

BRECHT: No, I wrote a German poem, but that is very different from this.

LAUGHTER

Stripling read some other excerpts from Brecht's writings and had the misfortune to be contradicted in his translation, not by Brecht, but by the interpreter from the Library of Congress. Then Brecht was questioned about his acquaintances and admitted that he knew the Eisler brothers, Hans and Gerhardt, one of whom (Gerhardt) had already been indicted for refusing to be sworn by the committee. Brecht also stated that Gerhardt had visited him during his sojourn in the United States.

"He used to ask for his brother who, as I told you, is an old friend of mine. And we played some games of chess. And we spoke about politics."

STRIPLING: Politics?

BRECHT: Yes.

CHAIRMAN THOMAS: What was that last answer? I didn't get the last answer.

STRIPLING: They spoke about politics. . . . Mr. Brecht, did you ever make application to join the Communist Party?

BRECHT: No, no, no, no, no. Never.

Thomas entered the questioning to inquire whether either of the Eislers had asked Brecht to join the Communist Party.

Brecht said no, that they had considered him a writer, not a political figure.

Thomas congratulated Kenny for his client, who had "done much better than many other witnesses you brought here," and then adjourned the morning session. For the afternoon, he promised the press "a surprise witness," who would link Hollywood with an attempt by Soviet spies to get information on the atom bomb out of the scientists at the University of California.

The surprise witness turned out to be Louis J. Russell, the collector of cards with code names, up for his eleventh time at bat in four days. His testimony had almost nothing to do with the announced subject of the investigation and was generally regarded as uninteresting, but it has a peculiar relevance to the mystery of Dr. J. Robert Oppenheimer's loss of his security clearance in a later and quite different political climate.

What follows is excerpted from Quentin Reynolds' account (*PM,* October 29, 1947) of the Russell revelations:

Russell talked in a low apologetic voice as if he knew he was disappointing his public. He told a long involved story which went something like this:

Louise Branston is a wealthy woman . . . once married to Richard Branston, who formerly owned the New Masses. *She often contributed to "communist front organizations." Russell testified that Louise was closely associated with Peter Ivanov, a Soviet consular official in San Francisco, and George Charles Eltenton, an employee of the Shell Development Corp.*

She was also friendly with Charles A. Page, a former State Department employee, now a free lance writer. Page (Russell said) was seen frequently with John Howard Lawson and Herbert Biberman. Now one night in 1942, Louise had a party. Among the other guests there was George Charles Eltenton and Haakon Chevalier, a professor of modern languages at the University of California.

Now according to Russell (who might have had a microphone in a cocktail shaker), Eltenton told Chevalier that Russia was our ally and how about finding out what was going on in the university laboratory so that he (Eltenton) could give that information to Russia.

Professor Chevalier thereupon went to Prof. Oppenheimer with a request for information. Oppenheimer (Russell testified) said that Eltenton's behavior was "treasonable." That was the story Russell told on the stand. He said that Eltenton was assigned by Soviet officials to get information about new destructive weapons. But Russell did not link any of the witnesses called to date with Eltenton.

In short, important as the information about Eltenton is, it hardly furthers the committee's contention that the Communist Party was infiltrated into the writing, directing, and producing of Hollywood pictures. None of the people mentioned in the long chain of events which led to Prof. Chevalier asking Dr. Oppenheimer for information, are picture makers. . . . The whole story had been turned over to the F.B.I. more than a year ago. . . . [T]he F.B.I. has taken no action against Eltenton or any others as a result of the information.

When Russell concluded his testimony, Chairman Thomas announced that "the first phase of the committee's investigation of Communism in the motion picture industry is ended." He did not say when it will be resumed.

That was the real surprise of the day.

When this abrupt and unpredicted termination was ordered, eight of the original nineteen had not yet been called. Spokesmen for the group and for organizations that had supported their stand exulted publicly. The Progressive Citizens of America issued an official statement which said, among other things, that "the adjournment was the first evidence that the committee has yet shown of any response to the will of the American people," and called for its abolition by Congress on grounds that its existence violated freedoms guaranteed by the Bill of Rights.

The committee ignored this and similar advice and proceeded to cite for contempt of Congress the ten men who had not been responsive to its questions. At the same time the Hearst press began a campaign for government censorship of films:

The need is for FEDERAL CENSORSHIP OF MOTION PICTURES. The Constitution PERMITS it. The law SANCTIONS it. The safety and welfare of America DEMAND it.

Liberals—especially liberal intellectuals—began forming ad hoc committees to "Stop Censorship" or "For the First Amendment," or "Freedom from Fear," or simply "of One Thousand." All were designed to fight the menace of censorship and to support—to varying degrees—the legal battle of the Hollywood Ten. The concern of this constituency was voiced by E.B. White in the *New Yorker* magazine: "The men have been convicted, not of wrong-doing, but of wrong-thinking; that is news in this country, and if I have not misread my history, it is bad news."

Unimpressed, Congress voted 346 to 17 to sustain the contempt citation and to turn the cases of the Ten over to the Department of Justice for criminal prosecution. On the same day, November 24, a meeting of the motion picture producers and the men who did their banking was convened at the Waldorf-Astoria Hotel in New York. Eric Johnston was present, and so was Paul McNutt, and so were most of the producers who had been called as witnesses in the hearings—most of them, incidentally, having been either begrudgingly co-operative or eloquently hostile.

The meeting went on for two days behind closed and leak-proof doors. When at last the doors opened, a spokesman announced to the press that the industry had reversed its position on blacklisting. There was a murky disclaimer of "any desire to prejudge the legal rights" of the men who had just been cited for contempt, but———

"We forthwith discharge and suspend without compensation those in our employ, and we will not re-employ any of the Ten until such a time as he is acquitted or has purged himself of contempt and declared under oath that he is not a Communist.

"We will not knowingly employ a Communist or a member of any party or group which advocates the overthrow of the Government. . . .

"In pursuing this policy, we are not going to be swayed by any hysteria and intimidation from any source.

"We are frank to recognize that such a policy involves dangers and risks. There is the danger of hurting innocent people, there is the risk of creating an atmosphere of fear. Creative work at its best cannot be carried on in an atmosphere of fear. . . ."

So unexpected and complete a capitulation by the industry

stimulated speculation about the cause. Ed Sullivan, who was openly sympathetic with the committee's objectives, wrote in the *New York Daily News* of November 29th:

> *Reason that Hollywood big shots rushed to New York and barred the ten cited by Congress: Hollywood has been dealt a blow that won't please Wall Street financiers, who have millions invested in picture companies. Wall Street jiggled the strings, that's all.*

There was some difference of opinion about who had won the first round of this battle. Most informed legal opinion was optimistic about the eventual disposition of the contempt cases, once the Ten had climbed the via dolorosa that leads to the U.S. Supreme Court. But the flank of a "free, democratically-oriented screen" had been turned by the institution of a blacklist. Dore Schary, a producer who had once been a screen writer and who had stood up valiantly under the committee's interrogation, was sent to a meeting of the Screen Writers' Guild to assure the membership that the producers intended to hold the line at ten victims, provided the Guild took no action in support of them.

The Ten needed support, not only from their guild, but from as wide a public as possible. They faced unemployment and unemployability, as well as awesome legal expenses. But they found it hard to rally support from fellow Americans who were unable to understand the curiously ambivalent position they had taken on the $32 and the $64 questions: whether they had refused to answer, and if so, why; or, if they had answered, what they had said.

Constitutional experts (of a liberal bias) wrote learned articles of explanation. Thurman Arnold, for example, held that in order to test the right of governmental agencies to inquire into a citizen's political and trade union affiliations, it was necessary first to phrase one's answers precisely as the Ten had phrased them; second, to accept a citation for contempt of Congress; and finally, to stand trial in federal courts and, if convicted, appeal to the U.S. Supreme Court. But to the lay public it came across as an unAmerican lack of forthrightness. "Why," the Ten were constantly being asked, "don't you just tell the committee to drop dead?" Or, "Why not come out and say what your politics are, if not to the committee, at least to the newspapers?"

Ring Lardner, Jr., tried to respond to this sort of question in an interview given to the *New York Herald Tribune:*

QUESTION: Are you or have you ever been a member of the Communist Party?

LARDNER: I do not wish to answer this question at this time for what seem to me to be congent and compelling reasons. . . . If I am a member of the Communist Party, I would be exposing myself to the bigotry and inspired hysteria which is forcing not only Communists, but all left-of-center political groups into a semi-secret status. . . . I would be banishing myself from the profession in which I have earned my living since I was twenty-one.

If I am not a member, I would be exposing other men to the same bigotry and blacklist by contributing to the precedent that all non-Communists must so declare themselves in order to isolate the actual offenders. Further, it would be clear to everyone, including myself, that I had purged myself in order to please my past and prospective employers.

Freedom of speech has no practical reality unless it includes the freedom to associate and act in concert with others of a like mind, and the freedom to keep to himself those opinions and associates a man doesn't feel ready to communicate to his neighbors. . . .

QUESTION: Why did you refuse to answer those questions when they were asked by the House UnAmerican Activities Committee?

LARDNER: I am not quibbling but speaking the literal truth when I say that I did not refuse to answer any question. The transcript shows that I was interrupted every time I started to speak.* What I did was refuse to submit to a yes-or-no limitation after the committee had given its "friendly" witnesses absolute latitude, including the right to make statements ten times as long and one-tenth as pertinent as the one I was refused permission to make.

I took this position for two reasons. One . . . was that I wanted to tell the committee that no one has to reveal what trade union or political party he belongs to, and the greater the display of force, the more I feel impelled to make this part of my answer.

---

* LARDNER WAS ONE of the witnesses who was forcibly removed from the stand.

QUESTION: Do you dispute or accept the authenticity of testimony giving the number of a Communist Party card and stating that it was issued to you?

LARDNER: To do either would be contrary to the position I have taken in answer to your other questions. But I think the committee's shy reluctance to let any witness, lawyer, or newspaperman get a glimpse of its "evidence" speaks for itself. And I would like to say that the one feature of the hearings that wounded me more than any other was the accusation that I—a man supposedly making his living by his imagination—would conceal my identity under the pseudonym of Ring L.

Kenny's explanation of his clients' evasive answers was that "it was a gimmick so we could get a crack at a jury on our way up. We didn't really think we were going to win till we got to the top. But we wanted to get the issue before a good old American jury, and the only way you can do that is to have a question of fact for them to decide. The question was supposed to be whether or not they refused to answer. What happened was that they would make a statement to the effect that the committee had no right under the First Amendment to be asking that sort of question in the first place; but the committee would say, 'All right, you said that. Now go on and answer the question.' And our men would make some more statements.

"What made it look pretty good as a question of fact—that is, arguable before twelve good men and true—was Thomas's short fuse. He kept blowing and having the witness taken off the stand before there had been much of a chance to answer, except by a yes or no.

"The trouble with a question of fact is that it can be decided either way. We didn't realize it, but no jury made up of government workers under the axe of Truman's loyalty purge was going to step out of line to decide our way. We had very good results with juries in California when we brought breach of contract suits against the studios that fired those men. But Washington was different. The good old American jury we got there had no trouble at all with the problem of whether or not the men had refused to answer." (RWK)

The Ten were convicted of contempt. Kenny, Margolis, et al., appealed. The Appellate Court sustained the conviction. By that time it was February 1949, a full year having been consumed in the legal process.

The Hollywood Ten with two of their lawyers. Front row (left to right): Biberman, lawyer Popper, Kenny, Maltz, Cole. Second row: Trumbo, Lawson, Bessie, Ornitz. Back row: Lardner, Dymtryk, Scott.

"We spent that summer working on our petition for *certiorari*, and we really thought we had that in the bag. It only takes four votes for *cert*, and we could count on Justices Black, Douglas, Rutledge, and Murphy. What we spent most of our effort on was organizing a lot of *amicus curiae* briefs. These are a sort of outside support, opinions filed by individuals who have some interest or presumed expertise. We had a very impressive list of people who signed them and were later blacklisted for having been 'friends of the court.'

"Then the grim reaper began to go after us. During the early part of the summer Justice Murphy died. And in the fall, Rutledge. I remember when I heard about Rutledge's death, it occurred to me that maybe our ball game had gone out the window. Tom Clark had replaced Murphy by then, and Truman proceeded to replace Rutledge with one of his old cronies, Minton of Indiana, and he was just dreadful!

"We went ahead and filed our petition (for *certiorari*) in October when the court convened, and then we waited every Monday morning from October 1949 to April 1950 to hear the answer. On April 10, I received a wire from Washington saying that *cert* had been denied, Justices Black and Douglas dissenting—that is, voting for it.

"The Ten went to jail on June 29, 1950.

"We had fought as hard as we could, and we had bought some time. Nearly three years of it. The Ten had held their fingers in the dyke from the end of '47 through most of '50. But as soon as they were in jail, exactly what they had been warning of began to happen.

"McCarthyism was let loose. Not only in Hollywood, of course. It hit every part of the country, every profession, every stratum of society. Lawyers found they had no more immunity than their clients. Why, at one time I found myself representing twenty-seven of my fellow barristers, along with twenty medical doctors, one optometrist, a dentist, and four osteopaths!" (RWK)

As the first snowfall of subpoenas hit Hollywood, so did news of the first recantations. It was by now clear that the blacklist would not be limited to the Ten. The hope of some, that if they could not work in Hollywood, they could pursue their professions in European film centers, had been blasted by the State Department's refusal to issue passports to persons whose travels abroad it deemed "not in the best interests of the United States." Economic pressure was raised past the level that many could tolerate. Some of the original Unfriendly Nineteen—even one of the Ten—began to inquire into the possibilities of purging themselves of contempt.

Kenny remembered that the first of the recantations shook him considerably. "It was a new experience, having one of my clients roll over. Of course, Larry Parks* was no longer my client. He had recanted in secret session (or executive session, which was the polite phrase) some time previously. But he was being forced to repeat his testimony in public and at a time, as it happened, when I was in Washington with the next set of vic-

---

* LARRY PARKS WAS a film actor who had been one of the most militantly outspoken of the Unfriendly Nineteen. At the time of his recantation, he had just appeared in the leading role of a film about Al Jolson, called *The Jazz Singer*.

tims. I remember one of the afternoon papers ran a headline which read:

JOLSON SINGS AGAIN!

"Larry objected to being 'made to crawl through the mud,' but the committee was adamant. He had to start naming names. That was the only escape hatch!

"Lots of people took it. The list of those named began to grow. And pretty fast, too, when the committee let it be known that re-naming those already fingered was not good enough. The monster needed a ration of fresh meat to stay alive and on the front pages.

"The '50s were really terrible. Some recanted, and some recanted their recantations. And of course there was Dmytryk, who managed to get his in while he was still in jail! I used to wonder later about Eddie. We'd seen a lot of each other during his trial—that was some time in 1948—because I had the use of an old friend's apartment in Washington, and Eddie used to come up there. We'd play gin and perhaps drink some. And I wondered afterward whether he had already begun making arrangements for more lenient treatment. He only got half what most of the others did.* Of course, if he'd made his peace before sentencing, he probably would not have gone to jail at all. But maybe he only made half a peace to start with.

"I used to wonder about Bart Crum, too. He was the lawyer who made the arrangements for Eddie. When did Bart decide to roll over? Not in time, I guess. He was in with the rest of us all the way up on the appeal. Of all the lawyers who took on the case of the Ten, Bart was the only one who shifted base. Poor Bart, he ended up having no friends on either side." (RWK)

---

* THE TEN WERE sentenced by different judges and served in different facilities. Eight were given sentences of a year; Herbert Biberman and Edward Dmytryk, who came before Judge Richmond Keech, got sentences of six months. Dmytryk served (as did Maltz) at an honor camp in West Virginia. The others including Biberman served at prisons in Texas, Connecticut, Kentucky, Missouri, and West Virginia.

10.
The Right of Silence

HE FLAW IN THE LEGAL DEFENSE OF THE TEN AP-pears, in hindsight, to have been their reliance on the protection of only the First Amendment. The assumption was that since that Article forbade Congress to make any laws abridging the freedom of speech, no legislative committee of Congress had a right to inquire into a citizen's political beliefs.

They could have backed up their defense by invoking the Fifth Amendment as well. But, as Kenny put it, "a lot of people thought you couldn't do that without using the word 'incrimination.' Since they didn't consider it would have been a crime if they had belonged to the Communist Party or the Screen Writers' Guild, it followed that the Fifth was of no use to them. And on that rather shallow analysis, everyone went to jail." (RWK)

It was during the research he undertook in connection with the appeal of the Ten that Kenny began to dig out the almost unknown history of the privilege and its roots in the oath *ex officio,* which was used by the English Court of High Commission and the Star Chamber for the rooting out of heresy, both religious and political. "What I discovered when I got into the books was that there were two distinct legal theories: the old Anglo-Saxon system under which nobody could start asking you questions until somebody had accused you of something; and the other, which derived out of the ecclesiastical courts. This particular ploy was called the oath *ex officio* because the assumption behind it was that the interrogator had the power to ask anything he wanted to because he had some kind of office. That's what *ex officio* means—'from the office.'

"The resistance to this sort of thing came to a climax in the early 1600s with a character called Freeborn John Lilburne, who was flogged through the streets of London, pilloried, and thrown into prison for his pains, with the eventual result that the Star Chamber was overthrown, the Stuart monarchs brought to their knees, and the right of silence enshrined in the list of basic freedoms guaranteed to citizens under both the British and the U.S. Constitutions.

"We used that phrase—the right of silence—in our brief for the Ten because they hadn't used the words, Fifth Amendment, on the stand. The government lawyer blocked that one by pointing out that the Fifth is a privilege, and you have to claim it. But after that we were on notice.

"The concept to be grasped is that the Fifth says no one in a criminal case shall be required to give testimony against himself. That's all it says. Nothing about being incriminated. And once we got that clear, it was simply a matter of educating people. Eventually, of course, we got our big ally in Dean Griswold* of the Harvard Law School. That helped make it respectable.**" (RWK)

That was Kenny's view. Ben Margolis, who was his colleague in most of the subsequent skirmishes with the committee, remembers it as anything but a simple matter. "There were real problems about persuading people to invoke the Fifth. One of my law partners was in violent disagreement with the whole tactic. He took the position—and so did a lot of other, very sincere people—that using it was tantamount to admitting guilt. He felt that people ought to get up before the Grand Jury or the House Committee or whatever tribunal was involved, and refuse to answer questions. Period!

* ERWIN GRISWOLD (later solicitor general of the U.S.), *The Fifth Amendment Today,* Harvard University Press, 1955.

** KENNY'S RESEARCH on the Fifth and the right of silence was the basis for a series of informal seminars held for the benefit of the recipients of the first set of subpoenas after the Ten went to jail, of which only rough notes remain. The same material was used in one portion of the Appeals Court brief on behalf of John Howard Lawson, and reappeared several years later (with the permission of the original author) in the dissenting opinion of Justice Jesse Carter of the California Supreme Court, in the case of the First Unitarian Church of Los Angeles, in the matter of its refusal to sign a test oath in order to preserve its tax exempt status.

In Appendix C there is a composite version of these two expositions, with some elaboration from notes taken at the 1950 "seminars."

"That was where Bob Kenny made one of his major contributions. He gave us an historical perspective on the privilege—its significance, its essential dignity. He did a scholar's job, and it made a tremendous difference."

The tremendous difference was that after the Ten, no one went to jail for failing to answer the entrapping questions.* But time after time during the next six years, men and women from the motion picture community and the community that had grown up around it were summoned before a House Committee on UnAmerican Activities and subjected to an inquisition that left them "at liberty" in the sense of having no gainful employment in their profession.

Successful screen writers became public stenographers in order to earn a living, or turned handyman or stock clerk in their wives' newly established dress shop or craft studio. Actors of both sexes—some who had been on the verge of stardom—learned to tend bar, drove taxis, gave diction lessons, or raised miniature trees for sale. On the whole it was easier for writers than for actors whose faces were too well known to be disguised.

Writers could submit their television and screen plays under assumed names or write for publication under their own names in other media. There was a thriving black market in which producers could hire or buy the finished work of top professionals at bargain basement prices.

The "Class of April 1951" (the first group to be called up after the Ten were jailed) consisted mostly of actors and writers. But subsequent classes included lawyers who represented clients in committee hearings, doctors, dentists, clergymen, university professors and grade school teachers, dancers, housewives active in the P.T.A. and Girl Scouts, stage hands and literary agents, secretaries, accountants, electricians, plumbers, and research workers. Some, though obviously not all, were subject to as cruel an economic penalty as motion picture professionals.

Marriages came apart under the strains imposed by these sudden changes of financial and social fortune. (There were circles in which battle stripes of this sort were not accepted as badges of honor.) Children developed reading blocks and other signs of trauma. There were exiles, "premature deaths from natural causes"—mostly heart attacks—and a few suicides.

---

* AT LEAST, NOT without deliberately setting out to test the efficacy of the First Amendment without the added protection of the Fifth.

But it would have been worse if the resistance had not been so stubborn and so imaginative, and Kenny's contribution to the resistance was considerable. He counseled class after class of subpoenaees, including the lawyers who represented them and were themselves subpoenaed.

Having established the efficacy of the Fifth Amendment as a way to stay out of jail, Kenny constantly explored variant positions that might keep an unfriendly witness from having to "wear the badge of unemployability" that was the price of invoking it. Not all those involved in the struggle approved of this effort, and Kenny was sharply criticized by those who believed that a unanimous refusal to yield even an inch of courtesy to the enemy would, in the end, establish the right of political privacy as a corollary to political freedom.

Opposing the purists was a group—not as large—that believed it was better to save as many livelihoods as possible, so long as that could be done without extending the committee's hunting ground by "naming names."

The trouble with the latter approach, in Kenny's view, was "that nutty decision in the Rogers case." Ms. Rogers was a Colorado Communist official who admitted under interrogation that she had been treasurer of the party. "But when they asked her from whom she had been collecting dues, she refused to tell them. She took the Fifth. The other side said she'd waived the privilege when she answered the prior question, and the U.S. Supreme Court upheld her conviction." (RWK)

There is a recognized legal principle of waiver that is usually applied in a civil suit when a witness has voluntarily appeared for one side or the other. If, after such a witness has completed making all the allegations he came to make, counsel for the other side starts to ask him questions, he cannot take refuge in the Fifth because he is then using it to resist the cross-examiner's legitimate effort to discredit his previous testimony. "The principle of waiver says, in effect, that a witness can't have it both ways, but obviously this doesn't operate in the same way when a witness is there against his will. What it meant in the '50s was that people who appeared before these committees had to walk a tightrope. They got so they were afraid to give their names for fear they'd be asked if they had ever used another name—a party pseudonym like Ring L. or Dalt T.!—and then when they'd try to take the Fifth, they'd be told they'd waived it by giving their names in the first place.

"Many people would have been glad to answer questions about their own political activity—they were proud of it!—but they had to clam up because they didn't want to be trapped into snitching on others, which is what got Ms. Rogers into trouble.

"It was the Rogers decision that permitted all those yahoos like Senator McClellan to go after a poor devil who was afraid to waive the privilege and ask him whether he'd committed one atrocity after another, and all he could do was say, 'I refuse to answer.' " (RWK)

Kenny and his law partner Bob Morris once worked out a tactic designed to get around this dilemma, a position they nicknamed the Half Nelson. Steve Nelson was a Pennsylvania Communist who had been summoned before a Senate committee and had answered the question about his membership, but had refused to discuss his activities or the identities of his fellow members. Nelson was not cited for contempt.

"Noting this, we worked out a position for a couple of our clients—an actress named Angela Clarke and a professor of film at U.S.C. named Andries Deinum—in which they said, 'Yes, I was once a Communist, and I'll tell you what I did. No, I'm not now. And no, I won't tell you about anyone else.' That was the Half Nelson, and they didn't get cited for using it, as they would have when the Rogers decision was operative. But Deinum was fired by U.S.C. and Angela Clarke was not engaged for any screen roles thereafter." (RWK)

Other variant positions were worked out by the attorneys for clients willing to go much further in appeasing the committee. These Kenny dubbed the Diminished, and the Augmented Fifths. "The Diminished Fifth was pretty popular for a while with those who hoped to wipe off the mark of unemployability. What you did was to admit that you were once a Communist but refuse to answer about whether you were now. (If you did that, you see, you were really in danger of having waived the privilege.) But it got a bit sticky because the committee's counsel was apt to push you around on how long ago you ceased to belong, attempting to create the impression that either you still were or had resigned five minutes before you were called to the witness stand.

"The Augmented Fifth was an even more desperate attempt to move the inquisitors to mercy. That was for the witness who not only answered about his past Communist Party membership, but threw in everything he could think of: bouquets for the committee, dead cats for his former friends and relatives, and so on. Named names! And then refused to answer when it came to the one about present membership. It never did its users any good that I was aware of. None of the clients I advised ever availed themselves of that one." (RWK)

Kenny's sobriquets for these two variants became part of the language of the resistance and served an important purpose, as did many of his other puns and wisecracks. Humor was a priceless ingredient in morale maintenance, and Kenny's bland irreverence expressed with spontaneous clarity the contempt in which this champion of the underdog held the top dogs of the day. Some of Kenny's most appreciated cracks hardly merit repeating, but they were repeated—and still are—like magic incantations for exorcising small devils.

An instance is the occasion when Kenny was representing twenty-two musicians subpoenaed by the House Committee and was heard by reporters to complain to one member that his clients were under suspicion of trying to overthrow the government by force and violins.

Another element of the resistance to which Kenny contributed was the institution of damage suits, most of them against the motion picture industry: its corporate entities, and the individuals who held office in them; but, in some cases, including as defendants members of the committee and its staff. Those of the Ten who were under contract when they were called subsequently sued for breach of contract. Kenny represented most of them. He won the first case, that of *Lester Cole* v. *Metro-Goldwyn-Mayer.* The Cole verdict, like most of the other favorable decisions in the lower courts, was reversed on appeal, in the climate of the '50s when the plaintiffs were all serving time in jail for contempt. The composite suit of the entire group against the industry as a whole was settled, out of court, for $140,000.

More interesting, and in the end of more significant effect on the blacklist, was a suit first brought in 1953 on behalf of twenty-three plaintiffs against the two associations of motion picture producers and the members of the House Committee and two of its investigators. This was a collaborative effort of Ben Margolis, Robert Kenny, and Sam Rosenwein aimed at finding some viable legal basis on which to fight the blacklist as an institution. The argument was that the industry and the committee had conspired together to deprive the plaintiffs of the opportunity to earn a living in the profession in which they had established themselves over a number of years. It covered men and women who had no contracts at the time they were subjected to the committee's ordeal. The lawyers had to "beat the bushes of Hollywood" for plaintiffs willing to have a crack at this backfire-setting. There was opposition among the blacklistees, particularly from those with the stature to command fairly good fees in the black market, and from some who had established themselves in other occupations in which any undue publicity might make new trouble for them.

Dalton Trumbo, for example, had stated publicly and frequently his belief that the blacklist would never be broken by a frontal attack on the producers. He argued—not without reason—that the producers did not like the situation any more than the victims did. His own strategy was to keep writing, keep his contacts in the industry green, and keep looking for a producer of courage who would, at some propitious moment, be willing to give screen credit to the anonymous writer whose work he had been buying cheap. In a sense events proved Trumbo's thesis, at least for him and a few other top talents. He won an Oscar under an assumed name, leaked his true identity, and exploited the resultant publicity.* But Trumbo's strategy was of no use to the majority of his fellow screen writers or to the actors or other studio workers who could not hide behind an alias.

"Something had to be done to keep people together," Margolis said. "There was no promise to anyone that we were going to win any substantial damages. (The amount asked was approximately $7 million.) Those were not the sort of times in which you could do that. But still you had to keep the fight alive, and this suit was one way to do it."

Eighteen of the twenty-three plaintiffs in what became known as *Wilson* v. *Loew's* were Hollywood professionals who had been called to the witness stand and had invoked the Fifth. Five of them had "been named as Communists before the committee and had failed voluntarily to appear and testify without invocation of the Constitutional privilege." In plainer words,

---

* TRUMBO'S ORIGINAL STORY for *The Brave Ones* won an Oscar in 1957 under the pseudonym of Robert Rich. No Robert Rich walked up the aisle at the award ceremonies to claim his golden image, and for months afterwards Hollywood buzzed with speculation about who and where the missing writer was. The producers, King Brothers, got screen credit for the story, the first time in Hollywood history, according to Trumbo, that a "yarn was written by a corporation."

they had not been found by the committee's subpoena servers at the time.

Among the twenty-three there were two Academy Award winning actresses, Anne Revere and Gale Sondergaard (who was the wife of Herbert Biberman of the Hollywood Ten); four screen writers who had been nominated for Academy Awards*; the collaborators responsible for most of the successful Abbott and Costello comedies; another writer, who had been known in the business as the "Queen of the Westerns"; a story editor who was also a distinguished American poet; a stagehand who had been active in studio unionizing; and a woman who had worked in the research departments of a major studio for over two decades. The state courts, both the lower and the appeals courts, threw the case out on the defendants' demurrers, holding that the Constitution did not guarantee any rights to people who had neither a specific work contract nor a reasonable expectation of a specific contract "in the industry from which he is excluded." This ruling had been more or less expected by the attorneys, and they promptly appealed to the U.S. Supreme Court, where they had little more hope of success.

Such appeals are costly, and the lawyers not only received no fees for their services, but also had some difficulty raising the money to pay costs in view of the general state of the plaintiffs' exchequers and the open opposition of men like Trumbo. But they persisted, and in 1957, to everyone's astonishment, the U.S. Supreme Court granted *certiorari* to the plaintiffs' petition alleging that by throwing the suit out, the state courts had acted in violation of the due process and equal protection of the law clauses of the Fourteenth Amendment. Such procedural errors, the petition argued, gave the U.S. Supreme Court jurisdiction. (Interestingly, this argument was derived in part from the McGovney argument on restrictive covenants. The question at issue was what constituted state, as against individual, action. McGovney had said that when state courts issued injunctions on behalf of privately convenanting property owners, or recorded deeds that contained such agreements, the action became state action. Margolis and Kenny were extending this interpretation to cover the sustaining of a demurrer, throwing a civil action

---

* MICHAEL WILSON, from whom the suit derived its title, was responsible for the screen play, *The Bridge on the River Kwai*, which won an Academy Award although his name had been removed from the screen credits.

out of court.) As an added argument they pointed out that the combination that had "denied employment opportunities" to the plaintiffs included members of Congress, which made it federal action in their view and established beyond doubt the jurisdiction of the high court.

The news of the granting of *certiorari* electrified the entire community. For the first time, the constitutionality of the whole witchhunt might be argued in the proper forum! "Substantial damages" granted to these plaintiffs might price the blacklist out of operation. And, as one skeptical plaintiff put it, "visions of sugar plums danced in the heads" of some of the twenty-three who had lived for four years or more close to the government's official poverty level. Trumbo and other opponents of the suit were converted on the instant and moved in to direct the planning of further strategy at meetings of the plaintiffs. Their opinion, shared by many of the twenty-three, was that such an opportunity should be capitalized upon by the addition of at least one prestigious name to the roster of lawyers who would make the final argument.

During the summer of 1957, Anne Revere was dispatched to the east coast to explore possibilities, and she came back with the news that it might be possible to persuade Joseph Welch to take it on. Welch was the Boston attorney who had appeared for the Army in the 1954 McCarthy hearings, and his performance before the television cameras had made him a national hero to those who had been cheering for the Army and/or against the Senator from Wisconsin. The difficulty was that Welch wanted $25,000 in cash and in advance and that he did not want to be publicly associated with any of the lawyers who had carried the case to this stage. He wanted "to walk into the Supreme Court alone."

At this point there occurred a split in the ranks, which is of interest because of what it demonstrates about the pressures on both lawyers and clients "at this point in time"—i.e., ten years after the first Hollywood subpoenas called Kenny back from P.C.A. business in Philadelphia. It can be understood only in the context of jail sentences served, careers broken, standards of living sharply reduced for people who had lived comfortably or better for most of their adult lives, an uninterrupted series of adverse decisions on all fronts, and the continuing threat of a nailed boot poised to deliver a paralyzing blow to one's solar plexus. In these circumstances the surprising thing about the

Wilson v. *Loew's* controversy is that it is unique in the history of the blacklist.

What happened was this: a meeting of plaintiffs was called to hear Anne Revere's report and the recommendation of the steering committee that had been conducting the plaintiffs' affairs. This meeting was better attended than was usual (it was hard to sustain interest in the on-going effort to raise money to pay lawyers' costs), but there were at least two absentees among the plaintiffs still living in Hollywood.* These two were informed by phone next morning that there had been a unanimous decision by those present to retain Welch, and that quotas had been taken for funds to be raised toward his $25,000 retainer. Also, it was mentioned in passing that Kenny would have to withdraw from the case to make room for Welch, but it was not made clear—if indeed it was clear to those in charge—that Margolis and Rosenwein were also to be dropped. It was stated in answer to questions that all three of the original lawyers knew and approved of this change of horses in midstream.

Someone checked with Kenny and was told that he had not been consulted, did not approve, and was in fact indignant at being pushed aside for a man who would be walking into the Supreme Court not only alone, but for the first time! As a result the two absentee plaintiffs and others who agreed to the change only because they believed Kenny and Margolis advised it refused to sign the letter of "contract" which Welch had stipulated must be unanimous. An acrimonious debate ensued.

One side—a minority—accused the other of deliberate misrepresentation of facts, of disloyalty to an honored champion of the cause of the blacklisted, and of fiscal irresponsibility. The pro-Welch faction was understandably outraged by this rebellion of the "irresponsible and ungrateful" rank and filers. Steering committee members had borne the burden of responsibility with very little help from those who were now throwing monkey wrenches, and had got nothing for their pains but apathy in the first instance and hostility in the second. They believed what they reported about the lawyers' assent to the maneuver to be the truth. And they were angry that this "last best hope" was to be jeopardized by a few penurious and pig-headed nonconformists.

* SEVERAL PLAINTIFFS had moved to New York, and Michael Wilson, who had managed to get a passport, was living and working in Europe.

Soon—but not soon enough—a meeting of all plaintiffs and all lawyers was called to air grievances and to clear the record. Ms. Revere reported again on her interview with Welch and on a subsequent conversation with Kenny, in which she thought he had acquiesced to his replacement.

"It was at this point that Bob blew," Margolis remembered with a certain awe. "In all the years I had known him I had never seen him really angry. He had always been the one who made excuses for people, played down any sort of personal feeling. But this time he just blew! He said he was being black-listed for having been prematurely anti-blacklist. And in a sense it was true. He had worn out his usefulness as a 'man of stature' by doing just this sort of thing—on the Smith Act appeal and a dozen or so others. It was just his courage and consistency that he was being 'punished' for. And he said a lot of other things that were completely out of character for him, such as being out of pocket for costs on the appeals of some of those who were advising the plaintiffs to go out and raise $25,000 for Welch! It was just an awful scene!"

The aftermath was an irreconcilable division in the ranks. One set of plaintiffs opted to stay with Kenny and Margolis, who had by now discovered that he, too, was to be dropped from the case and was unwilling to turn control of the argument over to anyone, including Welch. The other group was for hiring Welch if they could still get him, and someone else if they couldn't. A few days later, presumably unaware of this contretemps, Welch wrote that after discussions with other members of his firm, he was reconsidering his offer. He was not going to be able to appear on behalf of the plaintiffs, but he might be able to arrange for them to secure the services of a young and relatively unknown member of the firm at the same fee.* And before the plaintiffs could respond, he retracted even that offer.

---

* HALE AND DORR, of Boston. By an interesting coincidence, it was a "young and relatively unknown" member of this firm that provided some of the most dramatic moments of the Army-McCarthy hearings when the Senator revealed the fact that one of Welch's associates had once been a member of the National Lawyers Guild. Welch admitted that such a "youthful indiscretion" rendered the associate unfit for participation in the present case, but insisted that he ought not to be pilloried for an error of judgement that he had since expiated. Plaintiffs in *Wilson* v. *Loew's* were never able to learn whether it was this controversial member of the firm whose services were being offered them.

Hale and Dorr is, incidentally, the firm to which James St. Clair, Nixon's last Watergate lawyer, belonged.

The argument of *Wilson* v. *Loew's* was heard by the U.S. Supreme Court in March 1959. The brief, written by Margolis, was signed by Kenny and Rosenwein as well. The defendants were represented by M.G.M.'s counsel, Herman Selvin, whose argument prevailed with the court.

"He pointed out very effectively," said Margolis, "that if the Supreme Court ruled our way, every case would become a constitutional one, that is, every time a court threw a case out for lack of cause. The Supreme Court had been ready to extend the principle that the Fourteenth Amendment guarantees should cover such matters as a blacklist, as well as restrictive covenants, until they saw all the implications and decided that by God this would in effect end the sovereignty of the states. Besides, it would mean that they'd be absolutely swamped with work. So they decided that *cert* had been improvidently granted."

The $7,000,000 was up the flue.

But within a few months a new suit* based on similar grounds was filed, this one including the allegation that the "conspiracy" among the producers was in restraint of trade and therefore a violation of the Sherman Act, which meant triple, if any, damages. This suit was eventually settled out of court for a mere $140,000.

For some fortunate and talented artists, the blacklist was beginning to crack as early as 1957 when not only Trumbo's *The Brave Ones* but Michael Wilson's *Bridge on the River Kwai* won Oscars in their respective categories. The next year, 1958, an Oscar for the screen play of *The Defiant Ones* was accepted in public (and on television) by two men operating under pseudonyms, but clearly recognizable as blacklistees. In 1960, Otto Preminger hired and gave credit to Trumbo for the screen play of *Exodus* and work on the final version of *Spartacus.*

There was some premature rejoicing that the blacklist was broken. Frank Sinatra hired Albert Maltz to write the screen play of *The Execution of Private Slovik.* But Sinatra was part of the Kennedy inner circle, which was already working on John F. Kennedy's presidential campaign. The pressures applied were so extreme that Sinatra was forced to make a public recantation:

---

* KENNY was not associated with this second suit; Margolis was; and some, but not all, of the original twenty-three plaintiffs were the beneficiaries.

"I had thought the major consideration was whether or not the resulting script would be in the best interests of the United States. . . . But the American public has indicated it feels the morality of hiring Albert Maltz is the more crucial matter, and I will accept this majority opinion."

But Maltz was able to work profitably in Hollywood despite this setback, and eventually he and Ring Lardner and, of course, Trumbo were back at the top of their profession.

For others the thaw came too late. They had lost too many years.

In January 1975, the House of Representatives abolished its Committee on Internal Security, the revised and updated edition of the Committee on UnAmerican Activities, which was a revised and updated version of something called the Dies Committee, established in 1938. Thus, after thirty-seven years— or after thirty, if one prefers to count from the date of the establishment of HUAC as a standing committee of the House— and twenty-five years after the Ten went to jail for challenging the constitutionality of a congressional inquiry into the political beliefs and associations of citizens who had broken no law— the witchhunt was officially called off.

By that time Sam Ornitz and Herbert Biberman were dead. Adrian Scott lived only a few weeks longer. Trumbo and Lawson have died since. Bessie and Cole are still writing but have received no recent screen credits. Lardner and Maltz are the only two of Kenny's most illustrious clients still operating in Hollywood's much diminished motion picture industry.

Thirty years have passed since the institution of the blacklist, and there is no question that Hollywood's motion picture industry has lost the preeminence it enjoyed in the world of film. Many factors have contributed to this decline, but it is interesting that one of them was noted by the producers at the very moment they were announcing their decision to blacklist. They said on November 24, 1947:

"Creative work at its best cannot be carried on in an atmosphere of fear."

11.

The Defense of Dissidents

THERE WAS A PERIOD IN THE LATE '40s AND EARLY '50s when it wasn't clear whether membership in the Communist Party of the U.S. was a felony, a misdemeanor, or just economic suicide." (RWK)

The law to which Kenny referred in this statement was passed in 1940 and named after one of its sponsors, Rep. Howard Smith of Virginia. Signed into law by Franklin D. Roosevelt on the eve of the war, it required the registration of aliens who might be engaged in espionage or sabotage. The sabotage section was never successfully applied to anyone. What was applied was a provision forbidding—on pain of heavy fines and long imprisonment—the "teaching or conspiring to organize to teach or advocate the duty, necessity, desirability or propriety . . . of overthrowing by force or violence the government of the United States."

That section was first invoked in 1941 against a group of Socialist Workers Party members in Minneapolis, the best known of whom were the Dunne brothers, Grant, Miles, and Vincent, leaders of the Teamsters' local there. They were convicted, appealed, and were denied a hearing before the U.S. Supreme Court (which meant that the constitutionality of the Smith Act was not tested). Eighteen of them went to jail.*

Five years later, well after the end of the war, the Department of Justice moved against the national leadership of the CPUSA on the charge that "they had conspired with one another and with other divers persons" to reorganize the party as

---

* THE COMMUNIST PARTY was bitterly hostile to the Trotskyist SWP and did nothing to oppose this conviction. In some cases, local CP groups were on record as applauding it.

"an assembly of persons who teach and advocate the overthrow and destruction of the government . . . by force and violence."

The first group indicted included eleven members of the party's national board (*Dennis et al* v. *the U.S.*). They were tried in New York's Foley Square Courthouse in a trial that lasted nine months and ended in a conviction, based in part on some unusual instructions given by presiding judge, Harold Medina, to the jury.

In previous cases that touched upon the constitutionally protected right of freedom of speech, it had been recognized that there were circumstances in which this right of an individual citizen might be superseded by the right of the government to protect itself from destruction. The test to be applied was whether or not there existed "a clear and present danger" of violent or revolutionary overthrow.

Since there was no such clear danger present in 1948, it might have been assumed that the First Amendment protected the eleven defendants in their right to teach or advocate Marxism–Leninism (the theoretical underpinning of their recently reorganized party). But Judge Medina instructed the jury that it was a matter of law that there "is sufficient danger of a substantive evil" because the Smith Act had decreed this to be the case. Therefore, if the jury found that the defendants had intended to achieve the violent overthrow of the government, not "presently" but even "as speedily as circumstances permit," they were guilty.

The defense argued that the Constitution gave Dennis* et al. the right to assemble, organize, and propagandize in any way they believed effective, to gain any ends they believed desirable for the country—a position they constantly referred to as "principled," meaning that it posed, in their opinion, the fundamental constitutional issue.

They lost, were convicted, and sentenced to serve five years in federal prison. Worst of all, their appeals to the U.S. Supreme Court succeeded in bringing about what they had believed impossible: an affirmation of the constitutionality of the Smith Act.

With Dennis and his associates in jail, the Department of Justice declared open season on the political Left. Another group of seventeen national leaders of the CPUSA was indicted and

* EUGENE DENNIS, general secretary of the CPUSA at this time, died in 1961.

*Kenny with Dalton Trumbo (left) and ILWU Secretary-Treasurer
Louis Goldblatt.*

tried in Foley Square. Fifteen were convicted, lost their appeals,
and went to jail.

The lawyers for the defense in the first Foley Square trial
were convicted of contempt of court and also went to jail. So
did five state leaders of the party in Maryland. Another eighty-
two state leaders from California, Colorado, Connecticut,
Hawaii, Massachusetts, Michigan, Missouri, New York, Ohio,
Pennsylvania, Puerto Rico, and Washington were indicted. It
seemed likely that if all of these leaders went to jail, the government would move against the party's general membership. For
as the Smith Act was being construed in the courts, there was
no reason to believe that any of the 80,000 or more Communist
Party members in the U.S. was immune from prosecution although the party itself was still legal.

All of the trials of the state leaderships ended in conviction.
All the convictions were appealed. But only the California case
(*Yates et al.*) was accepted for argument before the U.S. Su-
preme Court. The defense in *Yates et al.* was based on an en-

tirely different set of assumptions from those of all the other defense strategies. In the other cases it had been assumed by both sides that the defendants were either guilty or innocent as a group. The prosecution alleged that the Communist Party had been organized (or more precisely, reorganized in 1940) as a "conspiracy to advocate the violent overthrow of the government." Therefore, if an individual was a member of the party, he was guilty of what the Smith Act had decreed to be a felony: i.e., conspiring to advocate, etc. The defense did not deny that all the accused were members of the party. What it denied was that the party was in fact a conspiracy. On this decision the U.S. Supreme Court's opinion in *Dennis et al.* seemed to uphold the Smith Act. Thus, the burden of proof became a matter of bringing into court evidence that the Communist Party did in fact "teach and advocate," etc. And the government's lawyers produced for that purpose a sampling of the classic literature of Marxism, as well as an assortment of more contemporary agitational writings by Communists.

As Kenny put it, "Those New York lawyers were so sure that the Smith Act was unconstitutional—regardless of what Judge Medina said about 'substantive evils'—that they let the government get away with dragging in a lot of old scrap books full of what Lenin had said and what Karl Marx had said 100 years before. Also, the defendants apparently felt that there was some sort of principle involved in sticking together. Solidarity or comradeship or all-or-none. It was laudable, but it landed them all behind bars.

"When they got around to California, however, they came up against a different kind of opponent. Ben Margolis was in charge of the defense, and he wasn't going to let them get by on that sort of a case. He insisted on facts! And there just weren't any. The California trial (*Yates, et al.*) went on for a long time—about four months as I recall—because every time anything that looked like a fact reared its head, Ben would move in and destroy it. He never got discouraged. The government kept waving its scrap books, and he kept on insisting that there had to be facts.

"I remember when we finally got before the Supreme Court, and Frankfurter took a look at the trial record, which was massive—it ran to something like twenty-five volumes!—he said, 'Do we have to read all that? Isn't there some error of instructions or something like that we could concentrate on?' I'll confess

I would have bought it, but Ben didn't. And finally Warren caught the scent.

"He began heckling the government lawyer a little, asking him for facts, and there just weren't any."* (RWK)

At this hearing (October 8, 1956), besides Margolis, who represented the majority of the defendants, Augustus Donovan, a conservative San Francisco attorney argued on behalf of two defendants, Al Richmond and Philip Connelly, who were editors of the *Daily People's World,* and Kenny argued on the doctrine of "collateral estoppel" as it applied in the case of William Schneiderman.

"I had represented Schneiderman in 1940 in a denaturalization case. (I always like that term; it makes me think of some form of non-potable alcohol.) The government tried to prove its case then by reading into the record old scrap books and pamphlets.

"When the case was appealed all the way up to the Supreme Court—not by me, but by Wendell Willkie—the Court ruled our way on the ground that the government hadn't proved that at the time Schneiderman was applying for citizenship and taking an oath of loyalty to the U.S., the Communist Party was devoted to the violent and forceful overthrow of the government.

"What I was there to argue in 1956 was that the issue had been decided sixteen years earlier. Frankfurter didn't like the analogy I offered about the guy that had been released from a mental institution and certified sane. He and his fellow justices came to believe that the decision in the first Schneiderman case didn't mean the same doctrines might not have other connotations in other times and circumstances.

"But it really didn't matter because what the case turned on was Ben Margolis's contention about facts. Once that was established, the prosecution had problems they just couldn't handle." (RWK)

---

* MARGOLIS AMPLIFIED THIS analysis of his strategy by noting that the indictment actually pled that the Communist Party was *used* as a vehicle by the defendants in an alleged conspiracy to advocate the overthrow of the government, not that the party *was* the conspiracy. "If you allow this difference, then it becomes a question of whether each individual defendant was or was not a member of such a group within the Communist Party, and that meant you had to separate the evidence and judge each individual defendant on the evidence that he had or had not participated in such a conspiracy."

Margolis's version of Kenny's role in the California Smith
Act case is different. He too dismissed the particular point that
Kenny argued as relatively unimportant.

"What Bob Kenny and Gus Donovan represented in that case
was recognition that basic American constitutionally guaranteed
freedoms were at stake. At that point, you must remember,
there was a very small group of lawyers who were carrying the
burden of defending all the victims of the domestic Cold War.
Sometimes people who got a subpoena from the House Un-
American Committee could get other counsel. But when it
came to avowed Communists, most lawyers felt the position
was too exposed.

"We felt we were fighting for basic and important freedoms,
but we were being pushed into the position of defending suspected enemies of the country. That was the whole thrust
of McCarthyism."

Both Kenny and Donovan by appearing in *Yates et al.* were
affirming the premise that defense of dissidents was defense of
the Constitution and therefore of the country. Donovan's appearance in *Yates* was his first and last such action. (He was
unacquainted with both his defendants and refused to have any
contact with them until after his argument, which concerned
itself entirely with the matter of freedom of the press.) But
Kenny's appearance was simply one more in a logically connected series of actions that had carried him to the crest of the
wave in the Roosevelt era and dumped him in the trough that
followed it.

"I'll tell you another way in which Kenny's role was important," Margolis said. "I've been in the Supreme Court many
times before and since that day in 1956, and I don't recall ever
having heard a courtesy extended to another lawyer like that
greeting from Warren to Kenny. I believe it may have made
a difference in how I spoke when my turn came. It certainly
made a difference in how I felt."

On June 17, 1957, the U.S. Supreme Court rendered a verdict in *Yates et al.* v. *the U.S.* that dismissed the defense contention about collateral estoppel as inapplicable, but accepted
three other major contentions: first, that the statute of limitations had run out on the charge of "organizing" the Communist
Party to do the work of a conspiracy; second, that the trial
judge's instructions to the jury had failed to make an important
distinction between the advocacy of violent overthrow as an ab-

stract principle and advocacy as an incitement to actual action; and third, that the evidence against the individual defendants was inadequate for conviction. In the case of the two editors and three other defendants, the Court ordered an acquittal; in the case of the other nine, the Court suggested that if the government could come up with better evidence than it had so far, it might institute a new trial.*

The government never did institute such new trials. As Kenny saw it, "They couldn't. The cases against all the defendants were dropped in the end and so were all the Smith Act cases that were being held up waiting for a decision in ours. That involved a lot of people in a lot of places. After the *Yates* decision, no one ever again went to jail on the conspiracy section of the Smith Act except that poor fellow, Junius Scales, in North Carolina. They had a lot of far-out stool pigeon testimony against him. I remember one item about a summer school he had attended where someone else had suggested it would be a good thing to carry a sharpened lead pencil in your pocket if you were going to a picket line where you felt you might need a weapon. I don't believe Scales was even accused of having made this suggestion, but according to the informer, he didn't oppose it. He didn't say, 'Don't pay any attention to that idea.' And on evidence like that, he was judged to have given assent to the advocacy of actual action.

"That became the new touchstone: actual action, not a philosophical approach to revolution or what not. That's what broke the back of the Smith Act prosecutions, and the credit for it goes to Ben Margolis. He saw the weakness in the Foley Square defense; he worked out a remedy for it; and he stuck to it all the way up, even when lazy old Felix wanted to beg off." (RWK)

The California Smith Act defendants were in agreement with Margolis's estimate of the significance of Kenny's participation in their final appeal. All felt that he entered the case at considerable sacrifice at a time when it took courage to associate oneself with the defense of so battered a constitutional principle.

"Don't forget," said one of them, "that the lawyers who de-

---

* THE MAJORITY OPINION was written by Justice Harlan. Justices Black and Douglas concurred in part but would have gone further in rejecting the government's contentions. Burton dissented only on one point. Brennan and Whittaker "took no part in the consideration or determination of the case." Tom Clark dissented entirely and wrote an opinion stating that he would have upheld the convictions of all. Excerpts from the majority opinion and that of Justice Black appear as Appendix D.

fended Dennis went to jail. It took guts for a Kenny to stand up in front of his old boss, Earl Warren, and remind everyone that he was defending a Bill Schneiderman for the second time!"

"He certainly didn't make anything but expenses in our case," said another defendant. "And I don't believe he did any better from his work for the Ten or the other HUAC victims.

"You have to assume he took on all those non-paying cases because he felt they had to be done and there was no one else to do them. As a matter of fact, when we first asked him to join our defense, he said as much—that he really couldn't afford it. We had sent someone to ask if he'd join Ben Margolis and the others—actually, I think we had only one other attorney lined up at that point—and Kenny said he was just getting back into private practice. That was in 1952, after the Ten went to jail. But he said then that if we couldn't find anyone else and we really needed him, he'd take the case.

"In 1956 we asked him to come in on the appeal—and things weren't much better for him financially than they had been in 1952—but he did.

"What we gained by having Kenny was not only the services of one of the most distinguished public figures and the sharpest legal minds around—a real student of the Constitution!—but the reflected respectability of a man of his stature. It reflected on the issue, not on us.

"What it says to people who don't know much about the legal aspects of a case, when they see a man of Kenny's stature standing up at a time like that and defending people like us, is that here is something non-Communists—anybody who wants to defend the good things in the U.S. Constitution—have a reason to fight for!"

What Kenny lost is hard to measure. Some of his old conservative friends like Raymond Peters believed that "the state of California lost the services of one of the best public servants it ever developed." Al Richmond, Smith Act defendant and ex-editor of the *Daily People's World*, came to much the same conclusion:

"If he'd kept out of things like the Ten and even more, our case—if he hadn't kept on representing Communists and people who stool pigeons and HUAC staffers said were Communists— I think the Democrats would have been glad to forgive him the shellacking he took from Warren. Other Democrats got beaten in that '46 debacle and they came back. Look at Pat Brown. He was running for attorney general—Kenny's old job—and he didn't make it. But a few years later he ran again and did, and he stepped from that into the governorship.

"Or look at Jimmy Roosevelt. He was actually on salary for HICCASP* which later became the nucleus for the third party movement, which was farther out than Kenny was ever willing to go. But Roosevelt—like Brown and a lot of others—cleaned himself up and was accepted by the Truman Democrats. All it took in those days was a little public redbaiting."

In Kenny's case, Richmond believes, it would have taken only a very small concession to the prevailing climate, "because the California Democrats needed him worse than he needed them. Remember, Bob Kenny had been the leading Democrat of the whole west coast region right up to the day Warren defeated him, and he was being talked about even afterwards as a presidential possibility. They had no one else with a national reputation and his sort of ability. Jimmy Roosevelt and Will Rogers were both coasting on their fathers' names, and that's not the same thing."

Ben Margolis used almost precisely the same terms in his analysis of the "sacrifice of Kenny's career." "Bob might have had to crawl a little, but then again he might not. If he'd just stayed out of things like the defense of the Ten and the Smith Act, he could have become again what he had been before—an important and useful member of the Democratic Party establishment. But he just didn't function that way. I don't know whether it's born into a man or the result of education. But there it is."

* HOLLYWOOD INDEPENDENT COMMITTEE of the Arts, Sciences, and Professions.

12.

A Guild of Lawyers

I N THE 1960s, THE CALIFORNIA STATE SENATE'S FACTFIND-ing Subcommittee [sic] published its reports on the "Communist front affiliations" of prominent citizens, listing Kenny as one who "worked in several fronts simultaneously." Examples submitted in proof included his membership in the American Civil Liberties Union, the Emergency Civil Liberties Committee, the International Association of Democratic Lawyers, and the National Lawyers Guild, the latter characterized as "the foremost legal bulwark of the Communist Party."

This description particularly annoyed Kenny, who told a reporter late in his career, "Sure there were Communists in the Guild. It also represented labor lawyers. It was the first national bar association with blacks in it. . . . It was a God-damn good outfit in those days when nobody else in the bar was speaking up for civil rights."*

Kenny's evaluation of the Lawyers Guild as orginally constituted is that it was the "foremost legal bulwark of Roosevelt's New Deal." "The notion of a national association of liberal lawyers was born as a result of the situation in 1936 when the 'nine old men' of the U.S. Supreme Court were blocking all of Roosevelt's progressive legislation, and the American Bar Association was cheering them on. At that time the A.B.A. was really the legal arm of the Liberty League.** It's just incredible, looking back now, what they were for and against! (Of course it's not so incredible when you realize that it was made up of those lawyers who could get to conventions on railroad passes.)

* *LOS ANGELES DAILY JOURNAL* (legal newspaper), Feb. 5, 1975.
** THE LIBERTY LEAGUE was an organization of conservative business and professional men—and politicians—opposed to the "radicalism" of Roosevelt's first-term legislation, and dedicated to his defeat in 1936.

Why, they even bucked the Child Labor Amendment. I remember Jerome Frank* making a speech in which he said that the A.B.A. was giving the American people the impression that the American lawyer was opposed to everything they were for.

"So some of the people around Roosevelt—particularly Tommy Corcoran** and Morris Ernst***—got the idea that what was needed was another association of lawyers that would support and work for progressive legislation and also look out for the interests of the vast majority of lawyers who were not being represented by those corporation counsels that made up the A.B.A. (There were 175,000 practicing attorneys in the U.S. at the time, and only 30,000 of them were in the A.B.A.) There were some preliminary meetings of interested individuals in New York toward the end of '36, and early in '37 the call went out to all those crossroads Clarence Darrows to come to Washington on Washington's Birthday and form a new organization." (RWK)

A temporary chairman had been selected at the New York meetings, in the person of Frank P. Walsh, chairman of New York's Public Service Commission. Over his signature there was issued an *Appeal to American Lawyers,* censuring the A.B.A. for having shut its eyes alike to the needs of the public and of the profession because "its concern for liberty has been secondary to its concern for property," and setting forth the objectives of the new organization as follows:

1) To make the Guild and its members truly representative of the best thought and traditions of the American Bar.

2) To protect and foster our democratic institutions and the civil rights and liberties of all the people.

3) To advance the professional work and economic well-being of members of the Bar.

* JEROME FRANK, then a Securities and Exchange Commissioner, later SEC Chairman. Speech quoted in the *Boston Globe,* Feb. 12, 1937.
** THOMAS CORCORAN, a lawyer who worked very closely with F.D.R. throughout his tenure, often "without portfolio." At this time Corcoran was a special assistant to the Department of Justice, engaged in the drafting of legislation.
*** MORRIS ERNST, a New York attorney, identified with F.D.R. as early as the latter's term as governor; later served frequently as the President's personal representative on missions to Europe.

4) To promote justice in the administration of the law.

5) To advise the public on matters affecting the Bar and its work, the organization and operation of courts, and other matters which affect the administration of justice to the public.

6) And to make the Constitution and the judicial and administrative agencies effective and well-working instruments for accomplishing the purposes of law as declared by the will of the American people.

Six hundred lawyers from all over the United States came to Washington in response to this appeal. "They were," as Kenny remembered, "top men in the profession and public life: judges, U.S. Senators, the general counsels of both the CIO and the AFL, Phil La Follette, who was then governor of Wisconsin, Harold Stassen, who was a year away from becoming governor of Minnesota, Bob Jackson, who was solicitor general (and later a Supreme Court justice), Jerome Frank of the S.E.C., administration people like Thurman Arnold and Adolph Berle of the State Department, and a rising young man named Abe Fortas, who was later appointed to the Supreme Court although it didn't stick. There was Judge William Holley, of Chicago, who had been a law partner of Darrow's. There was Dean Hastie of Howard University Law School and Thurgood Marshall of the NAACP*—all the leading black lawyers of the country, naturally, since they were barred from the A.B.A." (RWK)

George Davis, of California, who had been one of Mooney's attorneys, was responsible for Kenny's attendance at the founding convention. "I was then a superior court judge and thinking about running for the state senate. Davis told me he thought it would be a good experience and I'd enjoy it, so I went along.

"It was just a magnificent experience for a wide-eyed peasant from the West! I'd never even heard of some of these movers and shakers, but others were already familiar names even to California ears. (We didn't know much about Democratic Party

* WILLIAM HASTIE WAS the first black ever to be appointed to the federal judiciary when he was named judge of the U.S. District Court for the Virgin Islands in 1937. He served later as governor of the Virgin Islands. At present he is listed as senior circuit judge of the U.S. Court of Appeals for the Third Circuit.

Thurgood Marshall, then general counsel of the NAACP; later solicitor general of the U.S.; presently associate justice of the U.S. Supreme Court.

politics because we didn't have much of a Democratic Party in the state in 1937. But even Republicans were beginning to be aware of the men who had contributed to that tremendous Roosevelt victory of 1936 when he won every state in the Union except Maine and Vermont.) There were even some Republican delegates in attendance; Harold Stassen, for one.

"Somehow I turned up as chairman of the nominating committee. I suppose it was largely because I came from the far edge of the continent, so I was considered to be removed from the various sectional jealousies of the East and Midwest. At any rate, I got a remarkable exposure in the job. I became acquainted with all these luminaries we were nominating for office. And incidentally, there were no problems about obtaining the candidates' consent. Setting up that slate was like shooting fish. Everybody we asked said, 'Sure!' Everybody wanted to serve.

"We put up John P. Devaney, who was retiring as Chief Justice of the Minnesota Supreme Court, as our first president, and surrounded him with a fourteen member national executive board that included Governor La Follette, Senator Homer Bone, Jerome Frank, Elmer Benson of Minnesota, Congressman Maury Maverick of Texas, Malcolm P. Sharp of the University of Chicago Law School, Osmund Fraenkel of the A.C.L.U., Tom Emerson, Ruth Weyand,* and five incumbent judges. We hired ourselves an executive secretary, and everyone went home to Cleveland or Detroit or wherever to organize a local chapter.

"I had a hand in setting up the one in Los Angeles. We used as a nucleus a local group that called itself the Amidon Club after a judge from North Dakota who had made a national reputation when he refused to issue injunctions against labor unions. Our first chairman was Lester Roth,** who had just resigned from the superior court. We had venerable members of the local Bar, as well as many of the liberal younger set.

"It was not a difficult job attracting members. Devaney had made a speech about the purposes of the Guild that proved very helpful, something to the effect that the Guild was committed

---

* THOMAS EMERSON, then principal attorney for the Social Security Board; later associate general counsel to the Department of Justice and the O.P.A.; still later, on the faculty of the Yale Law School.

Ruth Weyand, an Illinois attorney, presently general counsel of the United Electrical, Radio, and Machine Workers in Washington, D.C.

** LESTER ROTH, prominent business and community leader; presently presiding justice of the Second Appellate District, Division 2, since his appointment in October 1964.

to the job of convincing the ordinary citizen that all of us in the legal profession were not their enemies, and to the promotion of legislation for the general betterment of the citizen's lot, and for the priority of human rights above property rights.* That was a very attractive formulation in 1937." (RWK)

During the first year of its life, the Guild established chapters in major cities across the country with a total membership of over 4,000; founded an organ, the *National Lawyers Guild Quarterly***; and started a number of committees to work on special fields of interest. One of these began a campaign for the creation of an office of public defender in all criminal courts, despite the A.B.A.'s contention that such an office would encroach on the preserve of private enterprise.

Another committee concentrated on the problems of labor law, organizing a number of regional conferences to debate drafts of a model wages and hours bill, a state labor relations act, an anti-labor-injunction act, a federal taxation bill, and the licensing of detective agencies. There was another Guild committee at work on the problems of low income clients. All during the first ten years of the Guild's existence experiments were under way (notably in the Philadelphia area) on ways of meeting the legal needs of people too poor to pay regular attorney's fees but not poor enough to qualify for legal aid. Neighborhood offices, staffed by young attorneys, most of whom were Guild members, worked in programs that were the precursors of the OEO legal services programs of the late 1960s, as well as of the field of practice now known as poverty law.

But perhaps the most impressive of all the Guild's achievements that first year was its effect on the A.B.A. Jerome Frank's hope that "the very creation of this organization may have a profound effect on the American Bar Association and that, in time, the raison d'etre for this organization may vanish as a result"*** seemed to be fulfilling itself. In January 1938, Justice

---

* THE *N.L.G. NEWS LETTER,* Vol. I, June 1937, quotes Devaney as follows: "The Guild is irrevocably committed to the promotion of social legislation for the better protection and preservation of human rights from those who would destroy those rights in the name and under the guise of seeking the protection of property."
** LATER CALLED the *National Lawyers Guild Review.* The first issue carried among other things, an article by Supreme Court Justice William O. Douglas (appointed, 1939), then chairman of the S.E.C.
*** JEROME FRANK, reported in the *Boston Globe,* Feb. 12, 1937.

Devaney was able to report that "the A.B.A. at its Kansas City convention abandoned its opposition to [the Child Labor Amendment]. We take credit for their change of face, and we hope it's permanent."*

Kenny also attended the Guild's second convention in Washington in 1938, and again was chairman of the nominating committee. This time it was harder to find a leading jurist willing to serve as president, but finally Ferdinand Pecora accepted the post. Pecora had just finished serving as special counsel to the Senate Committee that investigated J.P. Morgan and the "money trust," and he was considered quite a coup.

Under Pecora's presidency the Guild continued to work toward the objectives stated in its original prospectus, but the political climate in which the work went on was undergoing a profound change. The Roosevelt administration was becoming less concerned with domestic problems as its attention was drawn to the threatening situation in Europe. As war became a clear and present danger, the neutrality of America emerged as a controversial issue. Public opinion was divided on what some called the question of democracy vs. fascism, and others called isolationism vs. interventionism. In May 1938, the House Committee on UnAmerican Activities came into being under the chairmanship of Martin Dies of Texas. In November the congressional elections wiped out many of the Democratic victories of 1936.

As the administration proposed less and less progressive legislation, the Guild's original role in supporting New Deal programs began to shift toward that of initiating legislation, and there was a difference of opinion within the Guild about the propriety of this shift. More energy began to be directed toward the solution of purely professional problems. There were regional conferences on the economics of the legal profession and on problems of adminstrative law; Guild resolutions denouncing state censorship of films; a study of law schools in the District of Columbia, with the object of determining what kind of legal education students were receiving and how far it met the needs of the time. And there was pressure from a number of chapters for the extension of civil service coverage to all attorneys employed by the federal government, except those in policy-making positions. In January 1939, a Guild resolution formally called on the President to take such a step.

* JUSTICE DEVANEY, in a speech delivered in Toledo, January 1938.

The third convention was held in Chicago. Kenny recalled that "there was trouble starting up in the Guild, and I wasn't really hep to the reasons for it. I suppose it must have been the events in Europe. (It was amazing how much we were moved without realizing it by what went on over there.) This was the time when the French Popular Front was disintegrating in the aftermath of the Spanish War, and in this country there was a sort of pulling in of horns after those big Republican gains of the previous November. Dies had already started throwing his weight around, redbaiting here and there. And I suppose the fellows close to Roosevelt were saying 'We're going to have to keep an eye on this fellow and his committee.' It didn't bother us Californians much. We'd won big in 1938. But it did bother the men who had sent out the call to form the Lawyers Guild in 1936. They founded us in 1937 and dumbfounded us in 1939." (RWK)

The Guild was split over a resolution offered at the Chicago convention equating communism with Nazism. Debate was acrimonious. The resolution was eventually defeated, but by so small a margin that the "victory of the Left" was only a technical one.

"Joe Ball* and I had a big suite at one of the hotels," Kenny recalled, "and after that vote they all came up there—Pecora and Morris Ernst and Randolph Paul, the big tax expert—and there was all sorts of muttering about having to 'clean house,' terrible threats of resignation and stuff like that. I'd just been elected to the state senate back in California, and I didn't see any necessity of resigning from the Guild to keep my constituents happy.

"Just to show you how premature this sort of reaction was, it was at that same convention that Joe and I were entertained by Petrillo of the Musicians Union and the man who was later to become California's own Martin Dies, Jack Tenney.** Jack was in town as a member of the union on some business with Petrillo, and he asked Joe Ball and me if he could leave his bags in our rooms. We said, 'Sure.' So later on—when Petrillo de-

* JOSEPH BALL, prominent Southern California attorney, later president of the State Bar and fellow of the American College of Trial Lawyers.
** JACK TENNEY was at this time an officer of the Los Angeles chapter of the Musicians Union, whose international union, headed by Petrillo, was based in Chicago. Later Tenney held Kenny's old seat in the California state senate and headed what was known as the Little Dies Committee. Its "Guide to Subversive Activities" regularly listed Kenny as a fellow-traveller of Communist trails.

cided to throw a big party for Jack in our hotel—we got ourselves invited. It was really great. The whiskey was old enough to vote if it had had a mind to. And during the festivities Petrillo decided we needed some entertainment, so he called down to the hotel manager and said, 'Send up the band!' The manager was a little distressed; it seems they had a lot of people in the ballroom, dancing. But Petrillo said to send up the band, so they did. Louis Prima was part of the combo. That was very impressive to us western peasants, including Jack." (RWK)

The sessions that followed the debate on the plague-on-both-your-houses" resolution took up the matter of a president to succeed Pecora. "There was a lot of politicking in our smoke-filled room, and we ended up with a dear man named Gutknecht. He was a municipal judge in Chicago, and he was as innnocent as I was. He became our third president, and he pledged himself to hold the Guild together on the program we'd just voted in. Democratically! But the first thing that happened after that was Pecora's resignation from the Guild, charging Communist domination. I thought it was a kind of dirty trick to pull on old Gutknecht, who'd been hornswoggled into being president without any advance warning from the about-to-leave contingent." (RWK)

In the wake of the Pecora resignation came those of many administration-connected lawyers. Adolph Berle of the State Department was what Kenny called "one of the most earnest cleaner-outers." Others who left in the "snow-balling effect" that lasted through the rest of 1939 and 1940 included Robert Jackson, Thurman Arnold, Jerome Frank, Abe Fortas, and Arthur Goldberg. But Judge Gutknecht did not join the exodus. "It must have been a period of pure torture," Kenny said, "but he survived and ended up becoming District Attorney of Cook County" in Illinois.

Although the work of the Guild was severely impeded by these internal struggles, it continued to function under Gutknecht, taking public positions on foreign policy. One resolution urged the United States "to refrain from any action which may aid the prosecution of the invasion undertaken by the U.S.S.R. . . . and to adopt such policies . . . as will aid the Republic of Finland"*—hardly what Communist domination

---

* ON NOVEMBER 30, 1939, the Soviet Union invaded Finland, offering the justification that it was protecting itself against aggression from that quarter. In hindsight it appears that what Stalin was attempting to forestall was the use of Finland as a base for a Nazi invasion of the Soviet Union.

would have led one to expect. The Guild also adopted a resolution supporting the Geyer Anti-Poll Tax measure and resolved
to oppose bills under consideration in Congress that would have
set up concentration camps and legalized the deportation of
any alien advocating any change in the U.S. form of government. But for the most part, the Guild concentrated that year
on such unfinished professional business as the establishment of
a public defender system in the federal courts.

Kenny was elected president of the Guild at its fourth convention, held in 1940. His own comment is that his selection
"was more or less by default. That was a time when there just
wasn't anyone else." According to Martin Popper, then executive secretary, "There was no one else of Kenny's stature. He
was only a state senator, it's true, but he was considered a man
with a very big political future. Also there was no one in the
country as well equipped to heal the splits that had been occur-
ring. Everybody liked him. He could take a position and hold it
without making those who disagreed with him antagonistic. It
was a quality that was tremendously valuable to the Guild at
this particular time."

Kenny's first presidential "Message to the Membership," published in the *N.L.G. Quarterly* of July 1940, examines the role
of the organization in a period of impending crisis, both military and political. This article is one of the rare instances in
which his view of the responsibilities and role of a citizen who
is also a lawyer is set forth without humorous indirection or
diffidence.* He began by observing that the rise of fascism in
Europe posed a danger to the United States that "lies as much
in our attitude of mind as in the possibility of armed aggression." The lesson of Hitler's career, as Kenny read it, was that
"democracy was permitted to fail in practice long before the
destructive, anti-democratic forces prevailed." To apply that
lesson, America must "make the spirit of democratic institutions coincide with the day-to-day business of government,
economy, and social relationships. That business is primarily
the lawyer's business. It is peculiarly the business of the National Lawyers Guild." (RWK)

Kenny noted that the "lawyer has been rightly called the
soldier of civil life" with weapons that have been "fashioned by

---

* BECAUSE THIS MESSAGE states the philosophy that informed Kenny's career, both as a public official and as an attorney, it is reproduced
in full as Appendix E.

other lawyers through centuries of constitutional debate, legislation, and judicial exposition. Today as in other times of crisis,
the lawyer is being told that his arms were all right for dress
parade purposes, but too dangerous for practical purposes.
Thousands of American lawyers know that this is not so. They
know that the concepts of due process, equal justice, and
respect for human rights . . . are the best defense in the inevitable crises of the future. The National Lawyers Guild today is
the rallying point for every American lawyer who intends to
stick by the guns that society has entrusted to the legal profession.'' (RWK)

Specific proposals for implementing this awesome inaugural
included the defense of all progressive New Deal legislation
(social security, old age and health assistance, housing and agriculture), the defense and extension of civil rights and liberties,
and the "formulation of means toward [the] development of
an integrated economy, agriculture, and foreign trade which will
function democratically and for the maximum benefit of all of
our people, without special privileges."

This may sound like routine political rhetoric in the context
of a left-progressive tide in American politics. But two years
later, as attorney general of California, Kenny put into practice
an impressive number of these proposals, and offered his colleagues an object lesson in how a lawyer could serve as "the
soldier of civil life."

Kenny's first official action as president of the Guild was to
"go down to Washington to see if I could bring back those
strayed sheep of ours. It was not a very pleasant duty. Washington was terribly hot during the week I had chosen for my
shepherding, but I made the rounds—called on everyone I knew.
I called on Bob Jackson, who was attorney general by this time.
He was very glad to see me, and he said, 'Yes, you're right. We
all ought to come back.' So did Jerome Frank and most of the
others. It began to look as if the tide was running back in. But
all of them said, 'You've got to clear this with Berle.' He was
assistant secretary of state. So I go over to the State Department to see Berle, and he's not so sure. He says, 'Well, you're
clean.' (That was the word these people used to mean non-
Communist.) 'You're clean, but I'll have to check further about
these executive board members that have just been elected.'

"I said, 'You go ahead. I'm sure you won't find anything
that'll trouble you.' And I went back to my hotel, stripped
down, and got under a ceiling fan while poor Berle was busy

Attorney General Kenny plays the genial host to UN Charter Delegates in San Francisco.

applying the litmus paper to all the executive board and probably the office staff as well. It took him some time, but I was blissfully unanxious. In fact, I was elated. I thought I'd pulled it off.

"Then I get a call, and it's from Berle. The word was, 'You're not clean. You've got people who . . .' There was some indication of a willingness to bargain. I had the impression that a few resignations might have appeased the double-checkers. But I didn't think it worthwhile to pursue that course. I did talk to

Jackson again, but it was pretty clear we'd blown the duke. I licked my wounds and went back to California." (RWK)

All of Kenny's seven years as president were not as lean as this beginning suggests. "There was a real rapproachment after that day in June 1941, when Hitler broke his pact with Stalin and invaded Russia. Then everybody loved everybody again. Unity was rampant. Jackson came back into the Guild. Arthur Goldberg, and Thurman Arnold, and Jerome Frank—I don't recall all of our revolving door members, but I believe Berle was the only hold-out. Men like Supreme Court Justice Stanley Reid—and Rutledge and Burton and Black, as well—were all happy to attend Guild dinners and send wires of greeting and encouragement to Guild conventions. Why, we had so much prestige with the administration by 1945 that our president— that was me—and the president of the American Bar Association were both invited to Nuremberg to attend the War Crimes trials as official observers.*

"Even before that, when the United Nations was being organized in San Francisco, the Lawyers Guild was consulted. That was one of F.D.R.'s ploys. When he was breaking ground in a new field, he always 'consulted' everybody. There were forty organizations that got to have consultants in San Francisco. We had our own Consultants' Lounge, a pleasant place to chat, with free booze. Of course, no one consulted us much—neither the Guild's representatives, nor any of the other thirty-nine. Someone said we were the unconsulted consultants who met to determine the conditions of unconditional surrender." (RWK)

The full work record of the Lawyers Guild during Kenny's seven years as president is too rich and too varied to be covered here. It includes an attack on all the tasks set out in Kenny's Message to the Membership (cf. Appendix E): scholarly work on legislation needed by the majority of the citizenry; opposition to legislation that threatened "the practice of democracy"

---

* MARTIN POPPER accompanied Kenny to Nuremberg, and his account of the experience contains this observation: "The A.B.A. delegates were pretty stand-offish in social contacts with observers from the Soviet Union, but Kenny was a great mixer. I remember one official banquet where he proposed a toast, using that line from Robert Frost about 'good fences [making] good neighbors.' The Russians really dug that, and I've wondered since if that's when they began to think of Frost as our best poet and to invite him over so much."

in all areas of civil life, especially in those most severely threatened—organized labor and minorities. Labor's appreciation of the Guild's effort was expressed in a letter Philip Murray, of the C.I.O., addressed to Kenny in 1946, which said, in part:

> *For many years in the past organized labor has suffered most bitter experiences at the hands of attorneys who have considered paramount the interests of employers determined to destroy trade unions. It has, therefore, been of the utmost importance to our nation, and specifically to organized labor, that your organization has provided leadership in the legal profession in furthering progressive and humanitarian policies.* *

In the matter of discrimination against minorities, the Guild not only acted, but set an example that eventually forced the A.B.A. to open its membership to blacks. (The Guild's membership lists from the beginning included distinguished black attorneys, and one of them, Earl Dickerson of Chicago, served two terms as Guild president.) During Kenny's tenure, the Guild sponsored a national campaign against restrictive covenants, filed *amicus* briefs in suits aimed at outlawing the white primary, and sponsored a conference on the federal power to protect civil rights that laid the groundwork for what became, nearly two decades later, the civil rights legislation of the Kennedy and Johnson administrations. The Guild also protested and urged federal action against discrimination and violence directed toward Mexican-Americans in the Southwest.

This part of the record substantiates Kenny's claim that "the Guild was a God-damn good outfit in those days when nobody else in the Bar was speaking up for civil rights." But there is another part of the record that explains why, despite its admirable achievements, the Guild was about to suffer near-eclipse. During the latter half of Kenny's term, a second internal struggle rendered the Guild powerless to continue its programs or protect itself against attack.

One way of stating the difference between the two sides is to say it was a question of the proper function of an organization of lawyers in a democratic republic—the question Kenny had addressed in his first message as president. In the Guild there

* LETTER QUOTED IN full in the *Lawyers Guild Review,* May–June, 1946.

With Earl Dickerson, NLG president.

were "moderates," who believed it ought to concern itself only with matters relating directly to the legal profession and legislation. And there were "radicals," many of whom were Communists and most of whom were engaged in intense political struggles. They believed the Guild should express itself on the substantive political issues.

This latter position was not always a controversial one in the Guild. For example, in 1942 the Guild passed a resolution calling for the removal of Martin Dies from public life. (German radio was at the time quoting liberally from Dies Committee reports for its own propaganda purposes.) The anti-Dies resolution passed without serious opposition and set a precedent that was later used to propose and push through more controversial pronouncements. The most divisive of these was one condemning the Marshall Plan, offered for consideration at the 1947 convention.

One of the active advocates of that resolution was Ben Margolis, who later believed it was a mistake. "The Guild had

a large number of government lawyers," he explained. "Some had left in the 1939 split, but many had come back. And I remember their pleading with us not to pass that resolution. They told us they would have to resign. 'We work for the government, and that's administration policy. If it were a lawyers' issue, we might get away with it, but it's not that sort of issue.' And of course, they were right.

"I didn't see it at the time, but it wasn't hard to see later that we—those of us who pushed for it—made a mistake. The Guild had originally been formed as a sort of legal arm of the New Deal. What was happening in 1946 was that the New Deal was being transformed into Truman's Cold War deal. The relationship of government attorneys had to change. The Guild had to change—or split.

"Probably the split would have come anyway, sooner or later. But it would have been healthier for the Guild if it had been over a different sort of issue, one that was clearly the province of lawyers and an organization of lawyers. Bob Kenny took that position. He opposed the resolution. But when the majority voted for it, he accepted their decision. He didn't run out. That was typical of Bob. He felt that the unity of the Guild was more important than the particular issue or tactic."

Other combatants saw Kenny's acceptance of the majority verdict in a different light. A Chicago attorney who left the Guild at the time told this writer that "the people who passed that resolution—the pro-communist Left—didn't represent the majority of the Guild. They won by outlasting the rest of us. We had other things to do. We couldn't stay in those meetings until the last word had been said. Maybe Kenny wasn't on their side, but he wasn't enthusiastic in his opposition to them."

Clearly it was impossible to act as a non-partisan bridge between two ice floes caught in opposing currents.

The anti-administration resolution had precisely the effect predicted by its opponents. It started a second wave of resignations that peaked just before the advent of Senator Joseph McCarthy on the political scene in the early 1950s. By the time he was able to use Guild membership as a whip to beat opposing counsel in the Army-McCarthy hearings, the Guild's membership had fallen from 3,600 to 1,200. There were, of course, other contributing causes to this decline.

These were the days of the Taft-Hartley Act, the Walter-McCarran Immigration Act, the McCarran Internal Security Act,

prosecutions under the Smith Act, and the emergence of the House UnAmerican Activities Committee as the extra-legal arm of rightist political elements. Guild members took part in the defense of victims of all these instrumentalities, and the Guild took public positions in opposition to all of them. All this considered, it is perhaps surprising that the frontal attack on the organization was as long in coming as it was.

As early as March 1937, the attorney general of the U.S. was empowered by Executive Order #10450 to compile an official list of subversive organizations (no definition of subversive being included in the order). The Executive's authority to grant such power "to proscribe and destroy"* organizations was challenged in court, with the Guild submitting *amicus* briefs on the side of the challenge. But for a long time there was no indication that the Guild itself would be designated as subversive.

Then one day in January 1950, a news item appeared in the Washington papers announcing a press conference to be held by Clifford Durr** (who had succeeded Kenny as president of the Lawyers Guild in 1947), to release a report by a Guild committee on wire-tapping "and other illegal and offensive practices carried on by the F.B.I. . . . based upon the careful analysis of some 800 pages of F.B.I. reports introduced into the Coplon case."***

The night before the release of the Guild report on the F.B.I., Congressman Richard Nixon called the three major wire services and said he wanted to read over the phone the text of a letter he "had just dashed off" to the Chairman of HUAC (of which Nixon was a member), asking him to direct the committee's staff to investigate the Lawyers Guild as a possible Communist front. There was no time to mail copies of the let-

---

* FROM AN EDITORIAL in the *Washington Post,* July 1, 1948.

** CLIFFORD DURR, of Montgomery, Alabama, was the assistant general counsel of the Reconstruction Finance Corporation, and the architect of the Defense Plant Corporation during the war; later a Federal Communications Commissioner. After Roosevelt's death and the institution of Truman's loyalty program, he resigned and returned to private practice in Montgomery. It was Durr who arranged for the release of Rosa Parks in the action that triggered the Montgomery bus boycott, during which he acted as legal advisor to the Montgomery Improvement Association and its counsel, Fred Gray. Durr died in Alabama in May 1975.

*** AS REPORTED IN *I.F. Stone's Weekly,* Sept. 5, 1953. Judith Coplon was an employee of the State Department who was convicted of passing classified information to her Russian sweetheart. She had been under long and intense surveillance by the F.B.I.

ter, Nixon explained, because he wanted to be sure that the nation's press would carry the story of his "disclosures" in the same editions as the Guild's charges against J. Edgar Hoover and the Bureau. Which is exactly what he achieved.

The House Committee subsequently ordered an investigation of the Lawyers Guild and recommended to the attorney general that it be listed as subversive. J. Edgar Hoover announced his concurrence in that opinion. But the attorney general did not comply.

Not until Eisenhower appointed Herbert Brownell to that office was there action on the Nixon-Hoover demand. That came as an announcement by Brownell (in a speech to the annual convention of the A.B.A.) that he had been conducting a study of the Guild and was now prepared to make his determination public. "It has been clear," he said, "that at least since 1946 the leadership of the Guild has been in the hands of card-carrying Communists and fellow travellers," and he was on that day serving notice to the Guild to show cause why it should not be "designated." Two years earlier the U.S. Supreme Court had ruled that organizations could not be blacklisted in this fashion without some form of prior notice and a hearing. Brownell not only announced his intention in advance of such formalities, but also gave his reason for having arrived at what amounted to a verdict: "Communist leadership was evidenced by the fact that on every major issue the Guild has steadfastly followed the Party . . . line, excepting only those issues so notorious that their espousal would too clearly demonstrate Communist control . . ."; and that the Guild had defended Communists or opposed government action against them.

In the five years that followed, the Guild struggled to expose "the pernicious devices of guilt by association" and, in this case, "guilt by disassociation"* in conferences, pamphlets, and briefs

---

* A LAWYERS GUILD pamphlet, *An Appeal to Reason,* put the argument as follows:

Loyalty tests, as distinguished from the oath to uphold the Constitution which all lawyers have taken, have historically been employed as instruments of repression. Accordingly, the Guild has not inquired concerning and does not know the political beliefs or affiliations of its members. It believes that lawyers, like all other citizens, should be judged by their actions. . . . Condemnation of any group because of the affiliation of some of its members or leaders with other groups is an aspect of the pernicious device of "guilt by association" which [in the words of Prof. Henry Steele Commager] "is unsound because it assumes that a good cause becomes bad if supported by bad men. . . . [G]uilt attaches itself to illegal actions, not to dangerous thoughts or suspicious associations.". . .

(continued on following page)

amicus curiae. But no support outside the organization was generated as a result. No new members were attracted; old ones dropped by the dozens, and eventually by the hundreds. On the legal front, the Guild's effort was directed toward enjoining the attorney general from conducting the proceedings that would— foreseeably—end in its being listed. The first motion was lost in the District Court and appealed in a brief filed by Osmund Fraenkel, Joseph Forer, and Earl Dickerson. The brief in opposition was filed by Assistant Attorney General Warren E. Burger,* who had mapped the strategy of the government's prosecution of Owen Lattimore.** Several moves and countermoves later, on September 2, 1958, the attorney general's office consented to a dismissal of the case.

In a strictly legal sense, the Guild was never designated as subversive, never listed by the attorney general. But the object of the Nixon-Hoover-Brownell attack was achieved. Guild membership dropped to nearly 500. Publication of the *Lawyers Guild Review* was suspended. Only four Guild chapters (New York, Detroit, Los Angeles, and San Francisco) continued to function. Guild influence in the profession was virtually nullified.

Many of those who remained in the Guild were active in the civil rights struggles of the 1960s, and new student chapters attracted leaders that emerged from campus anti-war and free speech movements of the time. By the 1970s, this new cadre had begun to reactivate or "refound" Guild chapters in many parts of the country. Membership has continued to rise and many new programs have been initiated. But what has emerged is essentially a new organization with somewhat different goals and a very different composition. Membership is now open to all "legal workers" whether or not they have been admitted to the Bar.

The original National Lawyers Guild was a creation of the collaboration between the left and center forces that marked

(continued from page 138)
... [T]he Attorney General ... admits that the policies of the Guild in respect to important issues are in opposition to policies supported by the Communist Party. ... which should demonstrate to a mind open to reason the baselessness of [his] charge of Communist control. ... This is guilt by disassociation, based on conjecture.

* WARREN E. BURGER, later appointed Chief Justice of the U.S. Supreme Court by President Nixon.

** OWEN LATTIMORE, a State Department official, accused by Senator Joseph McCarthy of espionage for the Soviet Union; later cleared of all charges.

the Roosevelt era. It persisted as a defender of the values of the New Deal coalition when they were under attack by a coalition of right and center forces, frequently labeled "McCarthyism" although it operated effectively both before and after the Senator from Wisconsin's brief career. To the extent that those progressive values have survived in American political life, veterans of the Guild's first thirty-five years can take credit for distinguished service to the republic and to the Bar.

Members of the Los Angeles County Bar Association voted on April 24, 1975, to bestow the Shattuck-Price Award "for outstanding dedication to the improvement of the legal profession and the administration of justice" upon Robert W. Kenny. One of the speakers at the award ceremony was Joseph Ball, Kenny's old friend and fellow Guildsman. In view of the comparative youth of many of those present, Ball ran quickly over the history of those "years in the late '40s and early '50s when [Bob Kenny] was defending people accused of misconduct, disloyalty and so forth in our unfortunate land. . . . In those days of the Cold War, they set up loyalty boards throughout the nation. . . . The employees of government and industry were called before these people, and they were asked, 'What do you have to say for yourself?' The unfortunate employee would say 'Of what am I accused; who are my accusers?' The answer was, 'No comment.' Then in a few days they would get a notice that they had been declared disloyal; they'd be out of a job and, of course, blackened in reputation for the rest of their lives.

"Now a small group, all too small a group of lawyers throughout the nation undertook the defense of these people. One of these men was Bob Kenny. . . . It's sort of popular to do that now. I don't think anybody would look down their noses at anyone who would undertake the defense of an unpopular cause. But you have no idea of the feeling back in those Joe McCarthy days. I recall one time when [I was] on the board of governors [of the Bar Association] and a group of men came to us who had been convicted of a HUAC violation [sic] and asked us to get them lawyers to take their case to the Supreme Court of the United States. They said, 'We don't want lawyers who have any kind of red tinge. We want lawyers from the conservative Bar because we think they'll be listened to.' And then they told us a sad story. . . . [T]hey'd gone throughout this state and asked prominent lawyers, able lawyers, to take their case, and had been turned down because of the loss of reputation which threatened those lawyers if they took the cases."

It was in that context that Ball paid tribute to Kenny as "a man of independence of thought and action. A man who believes in the old fundamental freedoms," and congratulated the officers and members of the Bar Association for this "courageous advocate award that rights past wrongs [and] makes up for all the past sins against the principles of liberty, equality, and fraternity."

Ball and Kenny and a gallant handful of other charter members of the National Lawyers Guild may have been reminded at such a moment of Jerome Frank's hopeful prophecy that the existence of the Guild might so profoundly effect the American Bar Association that eventually its own reason for being would vanish. There was, despite the belated honoring of Robert Kenny, still a long way for the A.B.A. to go before the Guild could consider its mission accomplished.

13.

Infracaninophilia

WHEN KENNY RESIGNED FROM THE BENCH IN JANUary 1975, he was interviewed by a columnist from the *Los Angeles Daily Journal,* who reminded him of predictions of his political future made during the 1940s; for instance, Dean Jenning's *Coronet Magazine* article, published after the 1946 primaries in which Warren defeated Kenny, conceding that he would "not be California's next and youngest governor," but insisting that he was "just as likely to sit in the White House some day."

Kenny's comment was: "I always attributed that to the writer's wish to be kind to a wounded campaigner. I believed that no man who lost a gubernatorial campaign was ever going to make President. But since Nixon did the impossible, I've been forced to recall that there are no rules without exceptions. His comeback was the most remarkable escape from obscurity ever recorded. Perhaps mine would have run a close second."

The reporter went on to ask whether "in the light of the example posed by Nixon's success," Kenny was now sorry that he never re-entered politics. The answer was an emphatic no. "The human system is not made to regret things past," Kenny said. "I think of all the things I would have missed if I hadn't done what I've done."

Most of the things Kenny did during his first eight years out of public office were motivated by what his old friend and fraternity brother, Judge Fred Pierce, called "infracaninophilia. It's not my word, it's Bob's. Love of the underdog or something like that. It was a consistent pattern with him from college on. It got him in lots of trouble, particularly with the regular Democrats, as I learned when I was his campaign manager in

Sacramento in 1946. But in a sense it accounts for some of Bob's greatest contributions."

Later in life, Kenny might have called his course of action in this period "using weapons fashioned by other lawyers through centuries of constitutional debate, legislation, and judicial exposition" to make sure that "democracy did [not] fail in practice." Besides the defense of the Hollywood Ten and the appeal of the California Smith Act case, he was involved in a whole spectrum of resistance cases: the representation of other subpoenaees in hearings before congressional, state, and local Un-American Activities committees, and of the victims of school board inquisitions and immigration challenges.

Kenny was a member of the Committee to Protect the Foreign Born, and he defended many of its members in deportation hearings, among them Luisa Moreno Bemis.

Luisa Moreno was, in her youth, the leading poet of her native Guatemala. She came to this country in the '30s and became involved in the organization of food and tobacco workers, rising eventually to a vice presidency in the union—the first to be held by a woman. Later she married and retired to the life of a housewife. But the Tenney Committee on "one of its forays into San Diego County, subpoenaed her and returned her to the limelight." Soon thereafter, in January 1950, the immigration authorities started deportation proceedings against Ms. Bemis on the ground of past Communist affiliation.

"At the deportation hearings, the government produced an 'expert' on red ideologies, whom I prepared to cross-examine by having several quotations typed out without identifying the source. Some of them were Stalin's more conservative coexistence utterances; others were excerpts from A.F.L. union constitutions and One World statements by Wendell Willkie. The expert did exactly what I expected him to. He attributed Stalin's statements to Robert A. Taft and one of Taft's to Stalin." (RWK)

But despite Kenny's discrediting of the expert's testimony, Luisa Bemis was deported, her home broken.

Another lost case (with a happier ending) was the government's attempt in 1950 to have Harry Bridges, west coast longshore leader, deported on similar grounds. Kenny appeared in this trial as a character witness. He was presented by the defense as "the former attorney general, state senator, and superior court judge, presently a director of several corporations, and a lawyer in private practice." After his statement that to his knowledge Bridges's reputation for thrift, honesty, and integrity was good, Kenny underwent cross-examination by a young government prosecutor named Donahue. He was twitted with having been Schneiderman's lawyer in a similar case. Kenny replied that it was true and that he had been associated in that instance with another lawyer, one Wendell Willkie, subsequently Republican candidate for the presidency, and that their argument had been sustained by the nation's highest court. Donahue next produced a list of "organizations designated by the U.S. attorney general as subversive." Kenny claimed membership in several of them and said pleasantly that they were, in his opinion, "effectively working for peace and democracy," adding that in matters of this kind he paid no attention to the opinion of the then U.S. attorney general. Had he appeared at a certain public meeting of one of these organizations? Donahue asked. Yes, he had, "along with Colonel Carlson of the U.S. Marine Corps."

"Now deceased?" Donahue asked unpleasantly.

"Yes. And Frank Sinatra, now alive."

There was more of this sort of sparring, with Kenny landing most of the punches. Then Vincent Hallinan, Bridges's principal counsel, got a second shot at his witness.

"In view of the multitude of questions put to you just now," he said to Kenny, "let me ask you: are you a member of the Communist Party."

"No," Kenny said, "but some of my Democratic friends have accused me of being a Republican."

Then it was the prosecutor's turn again. He asked Kenny if it was true that he had once written to F.D.R. and asked that one of the government's previous (three) cases against Bridges be dropped. Kenny said it was true. Donahue wanted to know his reason.

It was one of those openings that Kenny called a "gopher" ball, and he "hit it out of the park." "Because I thought Bridges was being pushed around because he was an honest and incorruptible labor leader," he said.

Hallinan recalled years later that he had been irritated that day by the way Kenny reacted to the badgering of the government lawyer. "When he came off the stand, Kenny walked by the table and put his hand on the young punk's shoulder. Gave him a fatherly little pat! In his place I'd have taken a poke at him! One to the jaw that would have laid him flat!" Yet when

Hallinan's zeal in the defense of his client moved the judge to sentence him to six months for contempt, it was Kenny who appeared on his behalf in the appeal to the circuit court.

What Kenny recalled about the Bridges trial was walking out at the end of one session with Nancy Bridges, who was then Harry's wife. "Harry was walking ahead of us with Vince Hallinan and the associate counsel, McGinnis. Nancy says to me, 'I wish Harry'd quit going around with those lawyers. They're the only ones in this case who are going to jail.' And she was right! Harry's conviction was overturned on appeal, but poor Vince had to do his time in the pokey." (RWK)

Another, less-publicized case undertaken by Kenny in this period was that of a grammar school principal in Laguna Beach, a coastal resort city south of Los Angeles. This woman was subpoenaed by the House Committee in April 1953, and took the Diminished Fifth. She answered all questions about her political beliefs except those that touched on a period twelve years earlier (1935–40). She was not cited for contempt, but "from then on the bigots of Laguna Beach devoted all their time to devising some way to oust her from her job. They finally succeeded, but only after a court fight that took nearly two years." (RWK)

This type of delaying action Kenny later came to call "militant procrastination." He used it to good effect in the 1960 case of Synanon House and its founder, Charles Dederich. "Synanon was an organization of narcotic addicts, which occupied an old beach club in Santa Monica and was doing excellent work curing and rehabilitating addicts. Some neighbors protested their presence on the beach and got the cooperation of the Santa Monica authorities, who ruled that the group was in violation of some zoning ordinance. Or changed the zoning ordinance so that they were in violation. I forget the ploy, but it was something you could question.

"Anyway, Dederich was convicted and sentenced to serve thirty days in jail. We took the position that the ordinance—or the change—was illegal, and we appealed all the way up to the U.S. Supreme Court. Ultimately Dederich had to spend his month in jail, but by that time—thanks to my successful practice of militant procrastination—he had made Synanon a *cause celebre* and attracted wide support. I think he rather welcomed the short rest in jail. He had some writing he wanted to do." (RWK)

Another Kenny client who suffered harrassment unconnected

with Cold War politics was George McLain, organizer of a movement among California's old-age pensioners. He had sponsored, and won in the 1948 general elections, an amendment to the state constitution which, according to Kenny, "took the control of pension affairs out of the hands of county boards of supervisors and established a state agency, headed by one of McLain's devoted lieutenants." There is disagreement on whether McLain was an honest and effective representative of the pensioners, or an opportunist, trying to make a career out of their needs, but Kenny assumed the former. When the State Chamber of Commerce sponsored an initiative petition to repeal the McLain amendment, Kenny, acting without fee, represented the pensioners in an action to keep the repeal measure off the ballot. It did not succeed, but Kenny was for a time the "favorite son" of the pensioners.

The assurance of this sizable block of votes had something to do with his decision, in 1949, to try to regain his old seat in the state senate by ousting Jack Tenney from his incumbency.

Kenny filed early for the primaries, long before any other Democratic candidates had declared, and he collected a very impressive list of names on his nominating petitions. But months later, when Helen Gahagan Douglas and James Roosevelt decided to run for the U.S. Senate and the governorship respectively, they felt that their chances of victory would be lessened by having Kenny's name appear with theirs on the November ballot. (This was the period when Truman had established firm control over the national Democratic Party machinery, and on the local front Kenny was asking "What ever happened to good news?") A state assemblyman named Glenn Anderson was persuaded to give up his assembly seat and file for the senate. Since Tenney had cross-filed, this meant a three-way race in the primaries with an obvious danger that Tenney would win on the Democratic ticket as well as his own.

Kenny's law partner, Robert Morris, was present when Glenn Anderson and another state assemblyman called on Kenny, to explain the "general feeling" that his presence would weaken the ticket. Kenny was not ready to concede that he was a political untouchable, and he argued that he might bring strength to the ticket by reassuring a large segment of liberal independents who had voted Democratic through the Roosevelt years, but could not stomach Truman. Neither side was persuaded, but both agreed on the danger of splitting the opposition to

Tenney. Morris recalled that Kenny offered to toss a coin, cut cards, or throw dice to determine which of them should withdraw. "But they seemed to think this was a joke in poor taste and declined the gambit."

Tenney won the primary, was unopposed in November (except by the Prohibition candidate), and continued to represent Los Angeles County and to issue his "Guide to Subversive Organizations and Publications" for another four years. The absence of Kenny's name on the ballot did little to help either Ms. Douglas or Mr. Roosevelt. She lost to Richard Milhous Nixon by over half a million votes; Roosevelt lost to Earl Warren by more than a million.

Kenny's chagrin was deepened by the fact that his own private and hitherto infallible poll had showed him winning the nomination until a last minute saturation mailing by the regular Democratic organization on behalf of Anderson. Either because he believed that without intramural opposition he could still pull votes, or because his organization was "all tooled up and raring to go," Kenny decided to enter an even more ill-advised electoral contest that November. A petition for the recall of Los Angeles Mayor Fletcher Bowron had qualified for the ballot, and Kenny decided to try for the office.

His opposition to Bowron, who had been a friendly colleague in his judicial days, was an outgrowth of the Los Angeles City loyalty oath, which had been upheld by the state Appellate Court on July 19. A month later, Mayor Bowron went on the air to ask for "information about undesirables or questionable individuals . . . primarily those identified with or suspected of alliance with subversive activities. The names and doings of all persons suspected should be reported. . . . Let us get . . . the names, descriptions, habits and information about potential saboteurs. Let us know their associates, their activities. This will be one of the functions of civil defense, to lessen the effects of what our potential or actual enemy may do, either before or after actual hostilities."

This Cold War rhetoric was not as outré in 1950 as it sounds now, and it was an uphill fight to establish the position that in so speaking, Bowron was creating, not defending against, a threat to the practice of democracy. Kenny did not make it up the hill.

His comment, in retrospect, is that he was suffering from the disease *candidatitis*, whose symptoms include "delusions of invincibility," and from which the double exposure of 1950 cured him completely and forever.*

A few other samplings of gallant but lost causes of this period will fill out the picture. There were two important trade union cases involving—each in a different way—the applicability of the Sherman Anti-Trust Act to organized labor. The first case, soon after Kenny left the attorney generalship, was brought by the government against members of the Los Angeles local of the fishermen's union,** on charges of "acting in restraint of trade." Ben Margolis was attorney for the union, and he asked Kenny to enter the case "to do the scholarly work that gave us the guts of our defense: the historical concept that the anti-trust law was not originally intended to be directed against people like farmers or fishermen, people who were really at the bottom of the ladder with respect to power, who needed to combine to get even a minimal share. Bob did a great job. So good that we were able to use the material again in other connections. But unfortunately, there had been another similar case, in which the issues had not been made clear, that had gone up to the Supreme Court. That made it impossible to get our case heard there."

Kenny's argument met the same fate in the case of the Conference of Studio Unions*** against the major motion picture producers and the IATSE.† Kenny and his partner had spent a year preparing an anti-trust action on the theory that those groups had combined against the CSU and the independent motion picture producers "in restraint of trade." In this instance, it was a similar case brought by the Screen Carpenters that blocked the road. The earlier case had been argued and dismissed in a different federal court, and when Kenny's case came up, the judge followed that precedent and dismissed it.

When Ethel and Julius Rosenberg were convicted of delivering the secret of the atomic bomb to Russia and sentenced to

* KENNY EVENTUALLY had the pleasure of personally knocking out the Los Angeles County loyalty oath when he was a judge of the superior court. (cf. below.)
** UNITED FISHERMAN and Allied Workers Union, Local #33.
*** THE CSU, under Herbert Sorrell, was a militant, independent group of craft unions in the motion picture industry, opposed to what they charged was collusion between the rival union and employers group. They were frequently redbaited by spokesmen for both. Sorrell was personally attacked as a Communist or fellow traveller.
† THE INTERNATIONAL Alliance of Theatrical and Stage Employees (usually called the Stagehands Union), a strong, dictatorially-operated craft union, headed by a right-wing political leadership—roughly comparable to Petrillo's leadership of the Musicians Union.

death, Kenny associated himself with the movement to obtain clemency. He called on Cardinal McIntyre of Los Angeles to ask him to join the appeal. The Cardinal refused. "He told me not to worry. If they were innocent, they would go to heaven." (RWK)

Kenny also "lost a big one" on the international front in the bad year of 1950. He was retained in May to represent the People's Republic of China in an action to recover money deposited in the Wells Fargo Bank of San Francisco in the name of the Bank of China. The deposits, which amounted to some $750,000, were also claimed by Chiang Kai-shek's Taiwan regime. Kenny not only filed a claim, but undertook to introduce his client's commercial representative to San Francisco businessmen. The Chamber of Commerce was on record as favoring recognition of the People's Republic, and Kenny's diplomacy seemed to promise much. ("The resumption of the China trade would fill many empty American bottoms.")

On the legal front, Judge Louis Goodman ruled that the money should remain impounded in the bank until the matter of recognition was settled. Kenny and his clients were entirely satisfied with this ruling. "However, a few months later the North Korean episode changed popular sentiment. The federal appellate court returned the Wells Fargo case to Judge Goodman with a suggestion that he reconsider his decision in the light of the realities of current events. He did so. The deposits were ordered paid to the Park Avenue Chinese. My clients in Peking were offended by this and declined to appeal." (RWK)

It was a time for losing on the personal front as well. His "great expectations of inheriting the Walker fortune went up the flue" at a time when he could well have used the extra income, since most of his practice consisted of big ones that paid nothing but expenses, and not always all of them. He also lost a wife and a law partner. Bob's relationship with Sara, which had been strained to the breaking point, broken, and patched up, finally degenerated so completely that she quietly left the country "to represent the Baha'i faith" on the island of Madeira, and later in Nice. Morris Cohn, who had been Kenny's partner, speech-writer, and aide-without-portfolio during the attorney-general years, reluctantly dissolved his connection with the firm. The reasons may have been more economic than political; they were certainly not personal. Cohn continued to like and admire Kenny and told this writer that "some of my ideas have achieved a certain immortality by having been incorporated into speeches of his on which I worked. I'm proud of that."

Kenny's ability to handle alcohol, which had stood him in such good stead in the '40s, weakened under the strains of the '50s. During one of his electoral campaigns, he was arrested for drunken driving, and it was reported in the press that when the arresting officer explained that he would have to take Kenny into the station, the latter protested mildly that anywhere but in Los Angeles, a policeman who stopped him in such a condition would have taken him home instead. Some of Kenny's friends (and the culprit himself) deny that he was actually too drunk to drive on that occasion. His handling of a car under the best of circumstances gave the effect of intoxication, partly because of his bad arm, and partly because he was so frequently more interested in something not connected with the flow of traffic.

All in all, Kenny did not look good in these years. There were times when he looked almost seedy, his clothes going unpressed and even uncleaned for longer than they should in contrast to his normal, scrupulously neat grooming and soberly conventional dress (anywhere but in his Laurel Canyon retreat). And this was not because Sara's departure left him without the ministrations of a devoted female. There was a succession of wife-surrogates during the ten years that he and Sara were separated: all of them young, bright, and attractive; some more, some less interested in matrimony and baffled by Kenny's stubborn elusiveness. Women almost invariably liked him, before and after—or even when they never fell in love with him. He once told a friend that "the best friends I have I made in bed." Some of them, perhaps. But the remark fails to take into account his ability to make and keep the friendship of men.

He had by this time moved his residence to a small hillside bungalow, thirty-nine treacherously irregular cement steps up from a canyon cul-de-sac. There he kept open house—after his fashion—to any who could and would make the climb. A remarkable assortment of people did: young aspirants to public office, coming for advice from the man who couldn't win an office for himself; old school friends from Stanford and old "pollys" from Sacramento; radicals and reactionaries, trade unionists and bank directors; atheists and men of the cloth, like Father Ned Conway, Bob's Jesuit friend, whose proudest boast was that he forced the retranslation of Pope John's *Pacem in Terris* into English that "didn't cut the balls out of it." There were old friends and new ones and people old friends had sent with notes of introduction. There were blacks and Chicanos,

Europeans and Asians, distinguished and humble. They came singly and in numbers that seemed to threaten to tear his cottage off the decomposing granite hillside to which it clung.

The writer once attended what was billed as a dinner party chez Kenny. More guests than it was possible to count were packed into every square foot of floor and patio space. The kitchen was as crowded as the other rooms—full of people mixing or consuming Martinis and bull-shots—but there were no signs of preparation for a meal. Nothing more substantial than a few chunks of cheddar and some—but not enough—soda crackers were served during the first three hours of the festivities.

At about 9:30 there were some whispered colloquies among the wives of Kenny's associates, who seemed to feel some stirrings of a sense of housewifely responsibility. One woman asked whether the invitation had perhaps not been for dinner after all. Another went to ask her husband, implying that the invitation had been garbled in the transmission. But before consensus could be achieved, there was a shout of "Come and get it!" and all who could get close enough to the kitchen to look in saw the oven door thrown open, revealing about four dozen TV dinners piled in precarious disorder but piping hot.

"Assorted flavors!" said the host. "We cooked up something to please every taste."

It was not all fun and games, but it was not all gloom and doom either. Kenny lost more battles than he won, but he never seemed to question the efficacy of "keeping your finger in the dike." He never seemed to doubt that sooner or later— sooner, if he could help—sanity would return to the American body politic.

One small, but significant, indication of that underlying faith was a labor he undertook at this time and performed without interruption until he left private practice. At the end of each legislative session in Sacramento, Kenny prepared a digest of all bills passed into law. Prepared it, published it, and circulated it free of charge. It was easier for him than it would have been for anyone else because of his background, his ability to speed-read, and his phenomenal memory. But it was more than anyone else was willing to undertake or has undertaken since he stopped.

He did it for the fun of it, to keep his hand in something besides a hole in the dike, to keep in touch with the center where the action was and where he couldn't seem to stop wishing he was too.

14.

Back on the Bench

EDMUND (PAT) BROWN SERVED TWO TERMS AS GOVERnor of California, from 1958 to 1966. On several occasions during those eight years (most of them when he was in convivial company) Brown was heard to speak almost tearfully of his debt to "the man who gave him his start . . . to whom he owed his whole career . . . , who made him what he was." He had never forgotten, Brown said, that it was Bob Kenny who thrust him into his first race for state office, never forgotten the moment when the accolade fell so unexpectedly on his shoulder during the caucus to pick a slate for the 1946 campaign, when Kenny said, casually, "And Pat, you may as well run for the attorney general slot."

Unfortunately, Governor Brown did not feel himself in a position to repay that debt. Pressure was brought to bear on him throughout his term to appoint Bob Kenny to the bench, first because he was so eminently qualified and so obviously underemployed, and second because he lacked by six months the number of years of state service that would qualify him for a full pension, which it looked as if he was going to need. But every time it was rumored that the governor was considering such an appointment, there was a salvo from the Hearst press, the John Birch Society, and the organizations that "operated the anti-Communist fronts." Brown's political discretion always overcame his sense of indebtedness, and other arrangements were made to fill vacancies as they arose.

Kenny did nothing to make things easier for the governor in this respect. He appeared less frequently on behalf of "subversive clients" because his services were less frequently required. (Also, because he was no longer willing to serve as a "legal fig leaf" to make committee hearings look judicial.)

But his name appeared constantly in connection with such organizations as the Veterans of the Abraham Lincoln Brigade (of the Spanish Civil War), the Fair Play for Cuba Committee, Friends of the *People's World*, or the Committee to Protect the Foreign Born.

As Philip Connelly, once an editor of the *People's World*, put it, "His name was still on the letterhead of all those lost cause committees, any two of which was enough to get you blacklisted in the '50s. Kenny must have had his name on a couple of dozen! And he never turned down an invitation to one of those sad little banquets where they raise funds and hand out sad little awards. He seemed to feel a basic commitment to anyone who was still in there fighting. So if these tired old Bolsheviks got a charge out of seeing him up there, half asleep, on the speakers' platform, he was willing to put up with the warmed-over sliced turkey and peas and the interminable speeches."

It was not that Kenny didn't care whether he got a judicial appointment. He wanted it more than he was willing to admit, but it showed only once, when there seemed to be a good chance of his being nominated to the State Supreme Court. His old friend, Justice Jesse Carter, was plugging for him, and it looked for a while as if it were a sure thing. But Carter died in March 1959, and Brown filled that vacancy with another of Bob's old friends and admirers, Judge Raymond Peters. There was no more talk about the Supreme Court after that.

It was not until Brown lost his bid for a third term to Ronald Reagan in 1966, that he was able to summon his courage to offend the Kenny-hating sector of the electorate. By then he had little to lose, and it was clearer than ever that the state had much to gain by the appointment. Brown made the announcement, as one of his last official acts, that he was naming Robert W. Kenny to the Los Angeles Superior Court—the same one Kenny had left almost thirty years before to become a state senator. Once, much later, Kenny told an interviewer that he asked Brown for a place on the appellate court, but that Brown said he was too old.

Even at age sixty-five, Judge Robert W. Kenny was a nine days' wonder to a new generation of lawyers, clerks, and bailiffs in the Superior Court. Many of them had no idea that the moon-faced man in the "black muu-muu" had ever held any other office or taken the fire of Cold Warriors in other courts and hearing rooms. To this generation one had to explain, when one spoke of McCarthy, that the reference was not necessarily

Partner Bob Morris suits up Kenny for his return to the bench.

to the senator from Minnesota whose soubriquet was "Clean Gene," or that when one spoke of Wallace, the reference was not to the governor of Alabama.

Kenny's law clerks bragged about "this really great old guy" as if he were their own creation. He was, they claimed, the most popular judge in the County Building, partly because of his wit and partly because "he knows the law and how to use it; he's fair and he's fast. He can cut through a pile of briefs like a hot knife through ice cream, come up with the essential argument, and go into court ready to give judgement. And he sends people out of his court as close to satisfied as you can get in a law suit that has two sides to it."

I witnessed a typical Kenny performance in the Law and Motions Court. The session opened promptly at 9 A.M.—a novelty in this jurisdiction. The bailiff rose as the clock struck to announce that this was the Superior Court of Los Angeles County, Department 9, Judge Robert W. Kenny, presiding. Everyone stood. A door in the paneling of the back wall opened, and a short, red-faced man with sparse white hair carefully combed came in, sidled into the leather chair behind the desk, adjusted his half-glasses and peered affably over them, looking for all the world like a Gaelic version of one of the lesser Buddhas.

"We'll call the roll of today's cases," said Judge Kenny in a conversational tone. "Will counsel for both sides indicate their presence?"

It was a longish roll: thirteen cases. Figuring, from my own experience as a juror, an average of three-quarters of an hour per matter, I reflected that the morning's work load sounded more like a week's. But the pace was already breathtaking.

In four of the thirteen cases, one of the opposing counsel was absent and unaccounted for. On these the judge ruled "by default" and let the counsel who had showed up go on about other business. That took just five minutes. Nine cases remained on the docket.

His Honor asked next if there were attorneys present who had other engagements in other courts in the building. Three did. Two of these Kenny dismissed with permission to return when able. The third he offered to hear at once, "So you can be on your way."

The matter to be ruled upon turned out to be the wording of one of the defense motions, which counsel for the plaintiff found "personally offensive."

"Is that all that's bothering you?" Kenny looked at the other attorney. "Do you have any objection to striking that phrase? As I understand it, he's objecting only to the last six words on the—let's see here—on the fourteenth line. Can you get along without those?"

There was a pause during which defense counsel and Kenny read the line carefully. Kenny muttered, "I must say it does seem a little gratuitous. . . ."

And so a compromise was reached, and another case disposed of. Six to go, and the day's work was only beginning in most of the other courts along the corridor! The next to come up was a demurrer (a type of pleading that Kenny once described as a legal "so what?"). The judge consulted some notes he had brought with him and addressed himself to counsel for the defense.

"I'm going to let you go down all these allegations," he said with a slight edge of regret in his voice, "but you understand that you would have to throw out *all* the opposing side's arguments. In other words, you have to kill him completely. If there's anything left when you get through your attack, I have to deny your motions, and the case will come to trial."

I left the court for no longer than ten minutes, and when I returned, another pair of lawyers sat at the long table. Kenny was telling them that he had read their briefs, made his notes, and "just about decided how I'm going to rule." He looked over his glasses at the attorney for the defense. "In your favor. Which means you are in the painful position of having to sit down with a speech stuck in your throat. I sympathize. But there's no use taking your time and ours when I'm going to rule your way anyhow. Unless . . . " He turned to smile at the opposing attorney. "Unless you can change my mind. I've left it open a crack."

The attorney thus challenged got to his feet, cleared his throat, and picked up a thick, blue-covered sheaf of legal-size onion skin.

"You're not going to read all that, I hope," said Kenny in alarm. "I've done my home-work. What we need now is any *new* argument. For instance, it might help if you could explain to me what litmus paper you apply on the point of the difference between necessary and unnecessary services."

The lawyer seemed taken aback. He put down the brief, picked it up again, put it down, and began to riffle through it, stammering all the while that "we have several litmus papers here, your Honor . . . like on page 4, you'll find one where we contend that . . . uh . . . and another on page 5 and 6."

There was a snicker somewhere in the spectators' section, but not by so much as a twitch of his jowls did the judge indicate amusement at the poor man's discomfiture. Behind me someone was explaining the background of the case: something to do with a will by which the housekeeper-companion of an elderly man should have been—but was not—rewarded for unpaid services. This is, apparently, so common a phenomenon that the law takes account of it. Regardless of the provisions of the will and the existence of legitimate heirs, persons who can prove they have performed "necessary and substantial services" to the elderly cannot be cut off without recompense. Kenny's question concerned the services rendered, what they were and how they met the law's definition. Litmus paper was not a bad figure, but it conveyed nothing to the attorney, who was still rattling the onion-skin pages and suggesting that "if your Honor will read the brief we have submitted, you will find numerous examples of the—uh—kind of paper you mentioned."

Kenny's chin was sinking lower and lower into the neck of his robe. "Just a minute," he said at last and held up one gnarled, arthritic finger. The lawyer went silent, and Kenny turned to his law clerk. "Did you find that book I asked you to try and run down? Ah, good! If I may have it . . ."

A volume in a worn blue library binding was handed up, and Kenny fumbled through it till he found what he was looking for. He put a marker in the place and handed it to the unhappy attorney. "Here we have Griswold on the question," he said. "Maybe you'd like to look it over during the recess, and we could have another go at this later on."

"But your Honor, I've already prepared my citations." Someone behind me groaned quietly and muttered that "the damn fool doesn't know when he's being tossed a life preserver."

"I'm aware that you have," Kenny was saying, "but I still think this definition of yours could use a little refining and that this article may be of help. Of course, it may be almost unbearable for a Yale man to avail himself of the work of a Harvard law professor, but exercise your tolerance as best you can."

There was another ripple of amusement in the room, this time shared in by the lawyer, who was blushing with pleasure, not embarrassment. It was, after all, a mark of some distinction to be recognized by the man on the bench as the product of an Ivy League law school with old-school-tie antipathies to luminaries from a rival institution. (The lawyer, I learned later, was a partner of Jack Tenney's, which put the judge's generosity in a class with the pat on the shoulder of Bridges's prosecutor. Or so I thought.)

There were still four matters to be heard at eleven o'clock. As the next was called, a lawyer approached the bench and said apologetically that his opponent was on the telephone. "I've sent someone to call him."

Kenny lifted a disapproving eyebrow. "On the phone?"

"To his client."

"Ah! And there is some possibility that a settlement is about to be arrived at?"

The lawyer said there might be one before the case could be opened.

"I see," said Kenny. "Well, far be it from me to bring any pressure at so delicate a moment. I'll just get on with my homework. Let me know when you're ready."

He was making for the exit when a man stepped to the barrier and asked if he might address the court.

Kenny turned back. "You may."

"Referring to the record of yesterday, your Honor," the man interrupted himself to identify the case and continued, "it was written into the record, 'Court and counsel concurring.'"

"That's right. And you didn't concur, did you? I crammed it down your throat." He turned to the bailliff, a lady dressed in a rather gay print dress, and said gravely, "Let the record show: 'Ordered by the Court over the protest . . .'" He looked back at the lawyer and asked, "Vigorous protest?"

The man nodded, smiling gratefully.

"'Over the vigorous protest of counsel,' if you will be kind enough to make that correction."

The years on the bench were, on balance, happy ones.

Sara Kenny returned in 1963, slipping into her role as wife as unobtrusively as she had left it. But it was a changed husband with whom she was "reconciled," and the relationship that developed between these two, who had always been meticulously polite to each other but had found no common ground on which to build, was changed for the better. Sara was believed by some to have deserted Bob in his darkest hour. Her own view was that she had been deserted, within the appearance of a marriage, almost from the start. She had given up the appearance only when there seemed no other way to salvage the remnants of her self-respect. Now, for the first time, she felt able to offer and to receive affection, to perform small services and know that they were received gratefully, to share in at least part of "what goes on in that marvelous mind." She had always known Bob was brilliant, but she had not thought him wise. Now, as she told this writer, "He has matured in ways I never thought he could. And with all this wisdom and knowledge of himself and the world that he has accumulated, without dulling his intelligence— I tell you, I think Bob Kenny is just ready to begin!"

For Bob's part, he was restive for a while under the necessity to limit his choice of companions for dinner and the ball game in Chavez Ravine. (Sara was not a baseball fan, and he found that a serious flaw.) But he grew with astonishing rapidity "accustomed to her face," which was still beautiful, to her grace as a hostess, her skill as a *menagère*, and her dependable devotion. He was, perhaps, just ready to begin matrimony at last.

On the public front things were also going his way. Many of his old causes—the objectives of bills he had introduced into the state senate decades before—were appearing at last in the winner's circle. For instance, the death penalty, against which he had tried to legislate in his state senate term, was declared unconstitutional by the California State Supreme Court in February 1972.* The loyalty oath for county employees, which had irked him into running for mayor against Bowron in 1950, was invalidated in 1967 in an opinion he himself wrote. There was a howl of protest from the far right, which claimed among other things that Kenny was a sponsoring member of the A.C.L.U. when it brought the suit on which the opinion was rendered. But Kenny's view that the oath was unconstitutional was upheld by the California State Supreme Court.

The superior court is not frequently the arena for controversies of that order of importance, but it was noticeable that a large percentage of the "hot potato" cases turned up in Judge Kenny's court. The most sensational example was the conflict between Angela Davis and the regents of the University of California over her employment as a teacher in the philosophy department at U.C.L.A.—one which had ominous consequences for Kenny's continued employment as a judge.

The issues in this "first Angela Davis case" have been obscured by the melodramatic scenario of the second case in which she was involved. The background was the university's ban on the employment of Communists, first announced by the regents in 1940 and reaffirmed at intervals thereafter. On September 19, 1969, in pursuance of this policy, the regents dismissed Ms. Davis from a teaching position and forbade the granting of credit for any course taught by her while the dismissal proceedings were pending. In previous years, all the faculties of regional University of California campuses had either endorsed the re-

---

* IN NOVEMBER 1972, an initiative constitutional amendment to legalize the death penalty passed, 67 percent - 35 percent. But at this writing its constitutionality has not been ruled on by the state's Supreme Court.

gents' ban or kept a discreet silence on the subject. But this time, there were protests. The faculties at U.C.L.A. and San Diego voted to condemn Davis's firing. The academic senate at Santa Cruz called on the regents to reverse themselves. And, as if to atone for past apathy, the aroused lions of academe engaged counsel and prepared to bring suit against the regents, to enjoin them from dismissing the young black militant. They called upon the university's president and the chancellors of the separate schools to "act to make clear to California citizens the issues in the Davis case and the serious consequences to the university of regental harassment and intimidation."

On October 20, 1969, two such suits were scheduled for a hearing before Judge Robert W. Kenny. But before either of them took place, the regents had filed an "affidavit of prejudice" against Kenny and asked for a change of judge. No reason was given. When Kenny was questioned by the press, his comment was that he regretted the regents' action, but that since he himself was the author of the law that gave them the right to one peremptory challenge, he could hardly protest their exercise of it. He sent the cases down the hall to Judge Jerry Pacht, before whom they were argued, along with a taxpayers' suit to enjoin the regents from using any more public monies in an effort to oust Ms. Davis on grounds of her politics.

On December 26, Judge Pacht announced his opinion: the regents' declared policy of barring persons from teaching on the sole ground of membership in the Communist Party "constitutes a constitutional impermissibility and must be enjoined." He also enjoined the regents from using tax revenues to carry an appeal, restating Justice Jackson's celebrated dictum about the fixed star in our constitutional constellation, that no government official may prescribe what is orthodox. To permit the regents "to act as a political elite entitled to decide whose views are acceptable" would, he said, "be anathema in a free society." And he issued an order invalidating the withholding of credit for Ms. Davis's course in "Recurring Philosophical Themes of Black Literature."

The judge noted in closing that it was in the public interest that this controversy be settled as promptly as possible, "and in the courts, not the streets." In the light of what followed within the year, it seems that the public interest was poorly served by the regents' decision to institute an appeal despite his injunction against the spending of tax money to finance it.

Angela Davis continued to teach at U.C.L.A. until the end of that academic year. Her classes were well attended. But before the regents' appeal had been heard, the young teacher was a fugitive from justice, accused of having procured the guns used in a desperate attempt to rescue two black prisoners from their trial in a Marin County courtroom, in which one young militant, who had acted at times as Ms. Davis's bodyguard, and the judge in the case were fatally shot. Angela Davis was apprehended months later, brought to trial, and eventually acquitted. But her contract with the University of California had long since expired, and even her staunch supporters in the philosophy department did not attempt to press for its renewal.

Meanwhile, Judges Kenny and Pacht were subjected to a two-pronged attack from John Birch Society headquarters. On one front both men were threatened with impeachment by a resolution introduced in the state senate; on another, by a petition for their recall. If enough signatures could be obtained, such a proposal would appear on the ballot in November 1970. Kenny's situation was particularly sticky, for in the event that the recall should succeed, he stood to lose not only his position and salary, but the pension for which he had long since qualified. The accusations brought against both men were mostly gleaned from various Tenney Committee "Guides," including the charge that both had been supporters of the A.C.L.U.

The impeachment resolution was shelved in committee, but the collection of signatures for recall was carried on week after week by canvassers who were, by their own account, paid at the rate of a dollar per signature. When questioned, they had no idea who Robert Kenny was or what he was charged with. They needed the money; that was all. Discouraged in one neighborhood, they moved on to the next and continued their canvass.

After about a month, Kenny and Pacht were concerned enough to hire counsel. They were advised that the number of valid signatures required to qualify for the ballot depended on how the wording of the constitutional provision for recall was construed. The difference amounted to 234,000 signatures and might well constitute the margin between success and failure for the campaign. A suit was filed to obtain a court ruling on the question, but before it was decided, there was a rumor that the seemingly inexhaustible funds behind the recall effort had been shifted to another, more promising—or more threatening—sector of the Birch battlefront.

The final count did not show enough signatures to meet even the lower of the two target figures. The whole thing blew over leaving only a nasty taste in the victims' mouths and a bill for the services of counsel and filing costs.

Sara Kenny died in London, in September 1969, just before the fall term in which these controversies occurred. She and Bob had gone on their regular late summer vacation, first to southern France, where she had lived during most of their separation, and then to London, which was Bob's favorite city outside of California. She was stricken suddenly and died within the week. Kenny came home more shaken than he or most of his friends realized.

It was his law clerk who first noticed the difference: a marked drop in his old energy level, in the miraculous ability to read and digest a whole day's work in an hour and a half. He was approaching age seventy, the time at which he would have to retire, or take a 33 percent cut in his penison when he did. Kenny pondered his options and decided to go on working. But his health was failing, as might have been expected, considering the sort of abuse he had subjected his body to during the years when "it was a battleground of the barbitols": the pep pills to keep awake for long work (or play) sessions; the sedatives to put him to sleep when it was time to catch up; the drinking and eating too much and too richly; the stubborn refusal to make concessions to the onset of age.

Once he became so ill during a session that he had to call a recess, get a taxi, and deliver himself to the nearest physician of his acquaintance. He was sent to the hospital and emerged some time later minus a considerable section of his bowel. He was, as he told everyone, reduced to the status of a semi-colon.

But the puns did not hide the fact that he was losing his fight to hold on to the work that was now his life-line. He was determined not to resign at a time when Ronald Reagan would appoint his successor, so he ran for re-election in June 1974, and won—in the same election in which Pat Brown's son, Jerry (Edmund Brown, Jr.), was elected governor.

As soon as the new governor was installed, Kenny tendered his resignation. His health continued to fail, and on July 20, 1976, he died.

15.

The Undiminished Man

ROBERT W. KENNY'S CAREER IN PUBLIC OFFICE COVERS half a century, almost exactly the last half of the second century of the history of the United States of America. Few will dispute that it has been a discouraging phase of the great experiment in self-government that was begun in 1776. And seen against this background, Kenny's record—or image, as it is more popularly called—is peculiarly striking.

"He is one of the few men in public life of whom it can be said that he never once in his whole life made an opportunistic decision. He may be said to have sacrificed his career—as an elected official anyway—to that integrity." (Ben Margolis)

"He is a man of independence of thought and action, a man who believes in the old fundamental freedoms." (Joseph Ball)

"It will be written down that in this difficult time, he was not confused, and he was not afraid, and that he walked through difficult years with conscious morality." (Albert Maltz)

"Kenny is a true liberal, not a radical. He wouldn't last a week in a revolutionary situation. He's the type that always gets caught in the cross-fire. He's too cool, too relaxed about too many things. But incorruptible! And the remarkable thing about his sort of incorruptibility is that it's not just that he can't be bribed. He can't be scared either. It's part of his style, his off-hand, understated, uncompromising integrity. It's something that goes beyond principle. It has to do with roots." (Philip Connelly)

Stephen H. Fritchman, of Los Angeles's First Unitarian Church, also a Kenny client during the 1950s, summed up his view in an address at a banquet celebrating Kenny's return to the bench (January 1967):

> *... As we look at the so-called top people, the Establish-*
> *ments, the V.I.P.s in whatsoever group—presidents, gover-*
> *nors, senators, cabinet members, ambassadors ..., it's not*
> *only painfully apparent what they have paid to be there. The*
> *total exposure provided by all the media nowadays makes it*
> *clear, and even the unsophisticated can see, what has been*
> *chipped away, bartered off, watered down, smothered, in*
> *order that these types may gain what Shakespeare called*
> *"that bad eminence."*
>
> *After this unattractive survey, we turn around and look at*
> *Judge Robert Kenny. Even his worst enemies will concede*
> *that he could easily have made it to any of those bad emi-*
> *nences if he had chosen to diminish himself. Very many of*
> *his contemporaries and colleagues made this choice—this de-*
> *meaning choice. Judge Robert Kenny remains in a rather*
> *lonely but exalted spot. . . . . He is my idea of the perfect ex-*
> *ample of the Undiminished Man. He has refused to lessen*
> *himself.*

Why? Why should a man choose not to lessen himself if the
cost of that choice is defeat? Or, for that matter, why choose
to stay in a game where that is the almost inevitable result of
playing by the rules? Why not give up on American politics and
try terrorism? Or transcendental meditation? Or go back to
journalism, if that was truly the only profession in which Kenny
enjoyed himself?

I have suggested that Kenny's "style"—his nonchalance about
electoral contests—may have been the result of his indifference
to the outcome. But if that is true, it is true only of the contests
before 1946, the time when he couldn't lose for winning. It was
clear that he cared very much indeed whether he won or lost his
old senate seat in 1950. Even after he lost that election and the
next and declared himself cured of *candidatitis,* he was not cured
of his passion for political life. He simply indulged it in other
directions: in organizations like the P.C.A. or pressure groups
within the Democratic Party; in legal battles that were political
in everything but outward dress; and vicariously, through his
role in the careers of other, younger office-seekers who shared
his values.

It almost seems that the more he was defeated, the more he
was committed to the battle. Why?

A partial answer is supplied by Carey McWilliams (*see* Fore-
word): "One may be sure that Bob Kenny did not sacrifice his

political career lightly: politics was his life's blood. He did what he thought he had to do."

Another partial answer—or perhaps, a better way to phrase the question—lies in the possibility that what looked like butting his head against a stone-wall of rejection was actually a response to a different order of political reality. When a Robert Kenny, calling himself "the brave burnt child,"* chooses to invest himself in a political system that has been pronounced bankrupt by many of the best minds of his and the following generation, it may be that he perceives values in it that have been obscured, but not destroyed by those who have achieved "that bad eminence."

One interpretation of the message of Kenny's career comes from Dorothy Ray Healey, a Kenny client who was for 25 years chairman of the Southern California District of the Communist Party.** "Young radicals today are getting the same sort of oversimplified version of history that they got when I came along in the 1930s. They throw out the whole bourgeois democratic tradition and process as false. They don't stop to examine cases —and there aren't many as clear as Bob Kenny's—cases where someone actually carried out the ideas that bourgeois democracy always talks about, but rarely puts into action.

"That's what's significant about someone like Kenny, a man who stands when everything is going the other way. They can't stop the tide, but they slow it down. They keep the debacle from being too terrible. They don't have an easy time, and they aren't completely successful, but they preserve some things that can be used later. They keep something alive for the next generation of fighters."

This is true, of course, only if the next generation of fighters hears the news.

---

* KENNY USED THIS phrase as the title of a chapter in his manuscript dealing with the year 1950, in which he ran for office twice.
** "AS A MEMBER of the party's policy-making National Committee for 12 years [Dorothy Healey] was easily the most influential woman Communist in America, and even after her celebrated dispute with the national leadership led to her exclusion from the inner circles after 1969, she remained (until 1973) a dedicated party member and, to many, its most appealing and persuasive voice." *Ramparts Magazine*, Dec. 1973, p. 28.

APPENDICES

A. Earl Warren to Robert Kenny

Los Angeles
July 20th [1938]

Dear Bob:

I have not forgotten our recent discussion at luncheon and have not abandoned the idea of making a public expression of my views on the necessity of safeguarding our civil liberties.

I believe this to be the most fundamental and important of all our governmental problems, because it always has been with us and always will be with us and if we ever permit these liberties to be destroyed, there will be nothing left in our system worthy of preservation. They constitute the soul of democracy.

I believe that there is grave danger in this country of losing our civil liberties as they have been lost in other countries. There are things transpiring in this country today that are definitely menacing our future, among which are the activities of Mayor Hague and other little Hagues throughout the land. These activities are so basically wrong and so menacing to our institutions that every citizen and particularly every public officer should oppose them to the limit of his strength. As Attorney General I would do my best to prevent Hagueism from gaining a foothold in California. I am unalterably opposed to any species of vigilantes or to any other extra legal means of a majority exercising its will over a minority and I believe it is a base violation of trust to use a public office to accomplish the same purpose by observing the forms but not the spirit of our laws. I believe that if majorities are entitled to have their civil rights preserved they should be willing to fight for the same rights to minorities no matter how violently they disagree with their views. Further I am convinced that this is the only way they can be preserved.

I believe that the American concept of civil rights should include not only an observance of our Constitutional Bill of Rights, but also the absence of arbitrary action by government in every field and the existence of a spirit of fair play on the part of public officials toward all that will prevent government from using ever present opportunities to abuse power through harassment of the individual.

As a public official I have been and will continue to be guided in my actions by these principles.

With best wishes, I am
Sincerely,
Earl Warren

B. Robert W. Kenny to Professor Curtis D. MacDougall

July 13, 1953

Professor Curtis D. MacDougall
617 West End Avenue, Apt. 5–A
New York 24, N.Y.

Dear Professor MacDougall:

I am very happy to reply to your letter of July 5th. I will try to answer the questions you have raised.

As to your inquiry of the role of the Communists, my guess, from a purely California standpoint, is that the third party movement was just part of the misplaced militancy that developed in the left after the Duclos letter.

Wallace's band-wagon in California was ready-made for him. He came out here in 1947, after his European trip, as the editor of the *New Republic* and the man who had been kicked out of the Truman cabinet for urging a continuation of FDR's foreign policy. Inasmuch as the Democrats had taken a bad shellacking in the November, 1946, elections, it looked very much to us that Wallace could be right and Truman wrong. Before he got here the Hollywood Bowl cancelled his reservation for a meeting and this factor vastly multiplied public interest in his speech at the Gilmore Stadium on May 19, 1947. It was on this occasion that a big Hollywood collection was taken from Charles Chaplin, Cornelius Vanderbilt, and many film luminaries. The collection probably did not exceed $20,000, but the publicity magnified this sum at least ten times. (I am sure that it was this event which touched off the UnAmerican Activities Committee's "Hollywood Ten" investigation.)

Here was a candidate politically hot and capable of raising enough funds to make his venture feasible. The result was that when we had the Democrats for Wallace meeting in Fresno on July 19, 1947, it received national news coverage. (Perhaps this was accidental because it so happened that all the national political news writers were out here then on some kind of a Tom Dewey excursion. See *Newsweek,* p. 27, July 28, 1947).

You asked me why I "accepted the PCA chairmanship in Chicago in January, 1948, after Wallace had announced his candidacy in December." That is a sort of "When did you stop beating your wife?" question. Jo Davidson and Frank Kingdon were the original co-chairmen of PCA in December, 1946, when it was created by merging the NCPAC and the ICCASP. Jo Davidson resigned in July, 1947, when he went to Paris and I was appointed co-chairman in his place. (See *Time,* July 7, 1947.) When Frank Kingdon resigned in December, 1947, after some kind of dispute over a PCA executive committee recommendation that Wallace be urged to run as a third party candidate, I was then left as the boy on the burning deck.

> *"Kenny, who until Tuesday shared chairmanship of the PCA with Dr. Frank Kingdon of New Jersey, was in sole possession of the job yesterday. Kingdon, a Democrat and candidate for U.S. Senator, resigned as co-chairman of PCA immediately upon learning of the Wallace invitation.*
>
> *"In predicting that Wallace can win the Democratic nomination in California and other Western states, Kenny said:*
>
> *"'From the very outset, it has been the position of PCA that the voters should have some choice in selecting a President—that with Taft and Truman running, it would be like a professional wrestling match—a lot of grunting and groaning, but with the outcome never in doubt and of no particular significance to the spectators.*
>
> *" 'In California and other States where there are direct primaries, the plan is to run Wallace within the Democratic party,' "Kenny said; in States where party conventions choose candidates, he would run as an independent.*
>
> *"'My feeling is,' "Kenny said," 'that we are helping, not hurting the Democratic party. We're putting it back in the liberal column. We're taking it off the spot.'"* (San Francisco Chronicle, *December 18, 1947, p. 2.)*

During all of that time I was assured that the PCA had nothing to do with the third party and that was the general tone of the convention which followed in Chicago. However, no sooner had the convention adjourned than the PCA folded right up and went into the IPP.

Throughout all of this political cold war I never resigned from anything, which is some kind of a record. However, various organizations did resign from me, and PCA was one of them.

Relative to political strategy, my theory was that Wallace should try to capture Democratic delegations in those states where the electoral laws would permit him to do so, notably California, Oregon and Washington.

On the other hand, in those states where the Democratic apparatus was in the absolute control of a hidebound Democratic machine, it seemed reasonable to attempt something like the ALP in New York. I never felt that Wallace could be elected President, but it seemed to me that if he captured the West Coast delegation, a very likely prospect, he could probably dictate the choice of a Democratic candidate in 1948 and even if he could not, the progressive views of Western Democrats would have to be taken into consideration thereafter.

The reason I allowed myself the speculation earlier in this letter that there was Communist control is that I have always read that the Communists act on a blueprint regardless of whether or not the blueprint applies to the contour and terrain of the particular situation at hand. (The Draft Resolution circulated in January, 1953, seems to be documentary proof of this.)

Certainly the advice given to Wallace to leave his West Coast Democratic supporters high and dry must have come from people with absolute, inflexible minds, who thought that the progressive pattern had to be the same kind in every state of the Union. Perhaps Harold Young, now practicing law down in Odessa, Texas, can tell you something about this. He was much closer to Wallace than any of us then.

My trouble with Wallace always was bad timing. President Roosevelt did not want him for a running mate in 1944 and that was enough for me. I refused to join those who thought that Wallace was the answer in that year. The progressive Democrats denounced me roundly then. However, when 1948 came around, Truman's behavior and the martyrism of Wallace had made me a Wallace fancier. I am sure we could have held those progressive Democrats in line and beaten Truman in the California primary in June, 1948, despite Wallace's third party activities elsewhere.

As to my part in the 1948 campaign, the Democrats for Wallace Committee limped on after the IPP was formed that year but it was largely a letterhead, papier-mâché organization. We did not cooperate with the IPP because we regarded it then and now as a political mistake in California. You must recall that

the progressives controlled the Democratic party in California
in the elections of 1934 and 1938 and 1942, when Sinclair and
Olson were nominated for Governor. We needed a third party
here like a hole in the head. We had control of a second party
and might have remained in control had it not been for this
alien doctrine which came in from the East and dictated that
the left wing sever itself from the Democratic Party and go into
seclusion as a separate IPP. Such a move might have been wise
in Pennsylvania but it was utter folly in California.

I personally made several speeches for Wallace during the
1948 campaign and went on one statewide radio broadcast for
him late in October, 1948. But by then it was all pretty futile
stuff except for my Democratic enemies who used it to exclude
me thereafter from any Democratic Party activities out here. . . .

With best regards, I am

Sincerely yours,
Robert W. Kenny

C. *The Fifth Amendment*: Its Roots in the Oath *ex officio* and the Right of Silence.

(What follows is a composite version of the brief submitted in the 1949 appeal of *John Howard Lawson* v. *U.S.* and signed by all the attorneys for the Hollywood Ten; and the minority opinion of Justice Jesse Carter of the California State Supreme Court in the case of the First Unitarian Church of Los Angeles (1957) in the matter of its refusal to sign a test oath in order to preserve its tax exempt status. There are some elaborations of particular points taken from notes made for the discussion with prospective HUAC witnesses in 1950 and 1951, and some added material from the historical sources drawn on by Kenny in preparing the discussion.)

The notion that a human being has a right—sacred or secular—to privacy is as old as social living. One aspect of it is embodied in the maxim that a man's house (or tent) is his castle and inviolable. His mind and its contents were regarded as even more inviolable, and prior to the establishment of the right to express ideas freely, there was established in most societies of which we have knowledge the right *not* to express in public ideas or opinions best kept to one's self. The right to remain silent before one's accusers was relied upon by Jesus in his trial before Pilate (Matthew 26:62–4). Other examples from chronicles of distant times include an action of Alfred, the Great, in 890 A.D., reported in the *Mirrour of Justices*,

> *"... king Alfred caused ... to be hanged ... Seafaule because he judged Olding to death for not answering. ..."*

One of the most explicit rulings on the point was by the great British jurist, Coke, who took jurisdiction of the case of a man called Edward away from the ecclesiastical court which was trying to compel him, under the oath *ex officio*, to state the meaning of some allegedly libelous words, for the reason that:

172

"In cases where a man is to be examined upon his oath, he ought to be examined upon acts and words, and not of the intention or thought of his heart; and if any man should be examined upon his oath of opinions he holdest concerning any point of religion, he is not bound to answer the same."

A few years after Coke's ruling, the Court of the Star Chamber, under Charles I, began to use the oath *ex officio* in hunts for sedition, rather than heresy. The struggle that ensued reached its climax in the personal ordeal of one of the most remarkable figures in the long, rich history of man's struggle for individual liberty.

It began in England in 1638 when a young clothier's apprentice named John Lilburne (Freeborn John) was tried by the Court of the Star Chamber on the charge of having been involved in the printing and/or importation from Holland of a satirical pamphlet attacking the bishops of the Established Church.

Lilburne refused to take the oath on grounds that had by that time become standard operating procedure for Puritans and other dissenters who found themselves—if they did take such an oath—in an impossible dilemma. Essentially it was this: a man accused of "dangerous thoughts"—religious or political—had a choice between perjuring himself (and perjury was a sin as well as a crime) or exposing himself to penalties up to and including death, for beliefs or actions he considered to be obedience to the will of God. Such dissenting opinions actually were statutory offenses; religious and political freedom were not guaranteed by the law of the land, but on the contrary, unorthodox forms of worship, as well as criticism of existing political institutions and authorities, were punishable by law.

The right of a citizen not to be forced to incriminate himself, thus, was in essence the product of religious and political intolerance and persecution. The particular form taken by the struggle for that right had been—up to the emergence of Freeborn John Lilburne as its champion—resistance on quasi-religious grounds to the taking of an oath to answer questions truthfully.

Lilburne began his resistance on this familiar ground, already damp with the blood, sweat, and tears of a generation of plain people whose names are lost to us. He refused to take the oath because:

"a) it was not lawful according to the law of the land which allowed no man to accuse himself;

*b) it was not according to the law of God, which would
not allow a man to undo himself; and*
*c) it was not in accordance with the law of nature, which
expected every man to preserve himself.*"

Lilburne referred the irate members of the Star Chamber to
the example of Jesus Christ who, when asked to accuse himself,
said, *"Why ask ye me? Go to them that heard me."* (John,
18:20.) The Court was unmoved, and Lilburne and an elderly
co-defendant were both fined, sentenced to long prison terms
preceded by many hours in the public pillory, and, in the case
of Lilburne, an additional ordeal. He was stripped to the waist,
tied to the back of a cart, and flogged with a three-thonged whip
as he walked the long calvary from Fleet Street prison to the
New Palace Yard at Westminster.

The man ordered to execute this part of the sentence was
heard to remark that he had many times flogged criminals but
that this was the first time he had carried out the order on the
back of an honest and worthy man. The crowds that lined the
streets were of a similar opinion. They followed Lilburne to
Westminster not to mock and jeer him, but to share in the ec-
stasy of his martyrdom.

Despite the condition of his back and the agonizing position
imposed by the pillory, Lilburne gathered the strength necessary
to harrangue the crowd. He told the whole story of his arrest
and subsequent treatment, his reasons for refusing the oath, and
finally pulled from his pocket three copies of the booklet he
was accused of having smuggled into the country. These he
threw into the crowd and bade the people read the words to see
if there were in them "anything against the law of God."

A little late in the game, it would seem, someone was sent to
silence Lilburne. But a mere order to stop speaking did not
turn the trick. He had to be gagged, and it was done so brutally
that he began to bleed copiously from the nose. At this the
fury of the crowd against his persecutors rose another several
degrees, and there was a threat of serious civil disorder.

When his time in the stocks was over, Lilburne was thrown
back into prison, in solitary confinement, chained hand and foot,
untended despite a high fever, and all but starved to death.
Other prisoners smuggled him enough food to keep him alive,
and some one (or some ones) smuggled word in and out of prison. As he began to recover physically, he managed to get writing materials and began the composition of a whole series of ex-

traordinary agitational tracts, which were mysteriously conveyed to a secret press, printed and distributed in hundreds of copies.

It has been said that the whip that lashed Freeborn John smashed the Star Chamber and brought the Stuart monarchs to their knees. It is certainly true that in July, 1641, Parliament abolished both the Court of the Star Chamber and the Court of High Commission for Ecclesiastical Causes, and as a corollary, the oath *ex officio* on penal matters. It also, four years later, not only set aside Lilburne's sentence, but granted him a generous reparation for his ordeal.

But this was not the end of the matter. The basic right—that of a citizen to keep secret or freely to express views which might be unpleasing to authorities—was not yet established. Nor was Lilburne through fighting for it. As the forces headed by Cromwell took power from the king and the bishops, a new orthodoxy began to establish itself. Lilburne resisted it as stubbornly as he had resisted the oath, despite the fact that Cromwell had been his liberator, his friend, and his patron. For his part, Cromwell, unwilling to tolerate dissent from his own type of dissent, turned on Lilburne with at least as much fury as the Stuart Establishment had displayed.

The struggle took the rest of Lilburne's short life. There were victories and defeats. He spent more than half his adult life in prison, stood trial for his life four times, and finally died— at 42—in banishment. But Lilburne's real triumph and his enduring monument is a short passage embodied in the *Corpus Juris* which reads as follows:

"At some time, the date of which is uncertain, it became a settled principle of the common law that no one should be compelled to answer any question as a witness which would tend to subject him to a penalty or a forfeiture."
(70 C.J. 738)

The motives for invoking the right of silence by men like Lilburne are virtually identical with the motives that led other Englishmen of the same period to emigrate to the American colonies. It is natural therefore that, as Justice Hugo Black has put it (*in re Summers, 1945*),

"Test oaths designed to impose civil disabilities upon men for their beliefs, rather than for unlawful conduct, were an abomination to the founders of this nation. . . ."

Or, in the words of another justice of the U.S. Supreme Court,

"If there is one fixed star in the Constitutional constellation, it is that no official, high or petty, can prescribe what shall be orthodox in politics, nationalism, religion, or other matters of opinion or force citizens to confess by word or act their faith therein."*

If the first generation of "Americans" had been inclined to forget their forefathers' experience with test oaths and forced exposure of unorthodox opinion, there were soon enough new and purely American instances. The trial of Mrs. Ann Hutchinson, a heterodox, before Governor Winthrop of Massachusetts, in the year 1637, was recalled by Justice Black in another opinion (*Adamson* v. *California, 332 U.S. 46*):

". . . People with a consuming belief that their religious convictions must be forced on others rarely ever believe that the unorthodox have any rights which should or can be rightfully respected. As a result of her trial and compelled admissions, *Mrs. Hutchinson was found* guilty of unorthodoxy, *and banished from Massachusetts. The lamentable experience of Mrs. Hutchinson and others contributed to the overwhelming sentiment that demanded adoption of the Constitutional Bill of Rights. The founders of this Government . . . wanted to erect barriers which would bar legislators from passing laws that encroached on the domain of belief, and that would, among other things, strip the courts and* all public officers of a power to compel people to testify against themselves."

(emphasis supplied)

The history of the debates about the framing of this Constitutional Bill of Rights is available to any student of American history, but some of the background is not so easily come by. For instance, it is not generally known that twelve of the thirteen about-to-be-United States had already written state constitutions before the U.S. Constitution and its first ten amendments were framed. Nine of these state constitutions had separate bills of rights appended to them. The rights covered

---

* JUSTICE ROBERT JACKSON in *West Virginia State Board of Education* v. *Barnette* (1934), 319 U.S. 624,642.

in these nine lists were not the same in all cases. Certain rights now considered crucial and unarguable were missing from some. But the right not to be compelled to be a witness against one's self was in all of them.

Another significant point on which there is not much general knowledge is the matter of the precise phrasing of the right "against self-incrimination." In Madison's original draft of what became the Fifth Amendment to the U.S. Constitution it is put as follows:

> *"No person shall be subject, except in cases of impeachment, to more than one punishment or trial for the same offense;* nor shall be compelled to be a witness against himself: *nor be deprived of life, liberty, or property without due process of law; nor be obliged to relinquish his property, where it may be necessary, for public use, without a just compensation."*
> *(emphasis supplied)*

In the debates on this passage a lawyer from New York moved that the clause about being a witness against one's self "be confined to criminal cases." What he probably intended was to remove equity cases from this protection, but it is possible so to construe the phrase as to exempt also such non-judicial proceedings as the hearings of a congressional committee.

There was so little discussion of this suggestion, which was made and adopted with apparent carelessness, that it is possible to argue the intention of all concerned. But in the final version of the Bill of Rights, all clauses referring to the rights of a defendant in a criminal trial are grouped in the Sixth Amendment, and many constitutionalists (contemporaries of Madison, as well as those of our day) have considered that the principle—even with this restriction—is so clearly stated that it must apply to witnesses other than an accused, and to any stage of proceedings which might conceivably end in a "criminal" prosecution.

For example, as early as 1803, the privilege was argued in a case involving an effort by some Pennsylvania election officials to compel suspected Tories to give oaths regarding their past allegiance. The courts held this to be illegal and referred to language in the state constitution which is parallel to the language of the Fifth Amendment.

Alexander Hamilton thundered against a New York proposal to deprive former Tories of their property if they refused to take an expurgatory oath, and his language has been cited in our own day by Mr. Justice Field in *Cummings* v. *Missouri* (4 Wall. 277, at 330).

John Quincy Adams (then an ex-President of the U.S.) is quoted in the debates of the 23rd Congress (1832) on the same point:

> *"It cannot be within the competence of a committee of the House to institute a general search and compel the citizens on oath to purge themselves if innocent and criminate themselves if guilty, and bring with them their papers to be ransacked in a roving hunt for unspecified crimes."*

In 1839, in a proceeding that attempted to expose the secret activities of Masons in Pennsylvania by subpoenaing some of their members to testify against them, the ex-governor of the state was quoted in the *Gettysburg Compiler* (May 7), as saying:

> *"I have yet to learn that an inquisition at whose shrine the rights and liberties of the citizens are to be invaded is authorized by the principles of our institutions, . . . If no law has been violated, why call upon an individual to give evidence touching a lawful association? If unlawful, why call upon him to criminate himself?"*

Nor is this the end of the possible list. Unfortunately, rights have to be fought for over and over again. There are times—particularly in periods of postwar agitation—when the temptation on the part of officials and local governments to evade the guarantees of the Constitution on the rights of privacy are irresistible. Time after time, penalties of various sorts have been imposed—or attempted—on individuals who refused to disclose their past or present conduct and beliefs. While few have suffered to the degree of martyrdom, the right has only been reestablished at cost to those individuals who chose to defend it.

It is, therefore, an honor roll whose true claim to the gratitude of their fellow-citizens is too little acknowledged.

A further point which is frequently missed in this connection is the relationship between the right of privacy and the rights of association, speech, and assembly. Properly to understand this requires an understanding of the function of these latter rights in a democracy.

The powers of our government rest in a majority. Isolated opinion and purpose is not merely ineffective; it is a political zero; it does not have any existence. Even large minorities can act only by means of influencing representatives chosen by a majority.

The essence of the democratic spirit, therefore, is the opportunity for any one or more, unrestrained by government, to become a majority. (Italics added.) An agency of government which limits this opportunity is violating a major premise of the Constitution.

The rights to speak and to assemble are, of course, some of the means by which a man or an idea can win a constituency, perhaps a majority. These rights are secured, not only because they are valued by man as a beneficiary of government, but also because they are the means by which he can do his share of the work of government. And the freedom to assemble, or associate, and to speak out includes the right to do so in private.

Such rights would lose half their value if they could be exercised only in public. Ideas which were once as unpopular as American independence from the British Empire have, in time, won majorities. But premature publicity, at a time chosen by opponents (who constituted the majority at that moment), might have killed the fruit while it was yet in the seed. "One may be in possession of truth as of a citadel and yet be unable to defend it" if the enemy may choose the time of attack.

The time and occasion for challenging society by means of an unpopular opinion should be chosen by him who holds it, not by government. The dissenter may prefer perpetual silence or he may prefer the drama and risk of martyrdom. But the choice should be his, not the government's. To compel the choice is to impose as punishment for silent dissent the consequences of impious public challenge.

What is being defended by those who invoke the protection of the Fifth Amendment is, in effect, the last sanctuary—the ultimate refuge of every man. If a citizen cannot keep secret his difference with public officers, who would be safe and what life would be worth living?

Edward Livingston's impassioned argument in the last day of debate on the Alien and Sedition Bill speaks for 1948 as well:

> *The country will swarm with informers, spies, relators, and all the odious reptile tribe. . . . The hours of the most*

unsuspected confidence, the intimacies of friendship, or the recesses of domestic retirement, afford no security. The companion whom you must trust, the friend in whom you must confide, the domestic who waits in your chamber, are all tempted to betray your imprudent or unguarded follies; to misrepresent your words, to convert them, distorted by calumny to the secret tribunal where fear officiates as accuser and suspicion is the only evidence that is heard. . . .

Do not let us be told that we are to excite a fervor against a foreign aggression to establish a tyranny at home.

D. California Smith Act Decision

The opinion of Mr. Justice Harlan, concurred in by Justices Warren and Frankfurter; Justices Black and Douglas, concurring in part and dissenting in part; Justice Burton concurring in all but one finding; Justice Clark dissenting; Justices Brennan and Whittaker "took no part in the consideration or the decision."

U.S. Supreme Court Reports, 1957. pp. 1365 et seq . . . In the view we take of this case, it is necessary for us to consider only the following of the petitioners' contentions: (1) that the term "organize" as used in the Smith Act was erroneously construed by the two lower courts; (2) that the trial court's instructions to the jury erroneously excluded from the case the issue of "incitement to action"; (3) that the evidence was so insufficient as to require this Court to direct the acquittal of these petitioners; and (4) that petitioner Schneiderman's conviction was precluded by this Court's judgment in *Schneiderman* v. *U.S.* under the doctrine of collateral estoppal.

When it comes to Party advocacy or teaching in the sense of a call to forcible action at some future time we cannot but regard this record as strikingly deficient. At best this voluminous record shows but half a dozen or so scattered incidents which, even under the loosest standards, could be deemed to show such advocacy. Most of these were not connected with any of the petitioners, or occurred many years before the period covered by the indictment. We are unable to regard this sporadic showing as sufficient to justify viewing the Communist Party as the nexus between these petitioners and the conspiracy charged. . . . [I] t is upon the evidence in the record that the petitioners must be judged in this case.

We must, then, look elsewhere than to the evidence concerning the Communist Party as such for the existence of the conspiracy to advocate charged in the indictment. . . . [In the case of the five who were acquitted by this decision] the sole evidence as to them was that they had long been members, officers, or functionaries of the Communist Party of California; and that standing alone, . . . makes out no case against them. So far as this record shows, none of them was engaged in or been associated with any but what appear to have been wholly lawful activities, or has ever made a single remark or been present when someone else made a remark which would tend to prove the charges against them. . . . [On the *Daily People's World*] nothing in the material introduced into evidence from the newspaper . . . advances the Government's case.

[In the case of the remaining nine defendants] . . . while the record contains evidence of little more than a general program of educational activity by the Communist Party which included advocacy of violence as a theoretical matter, we are not prepared to say, at this state of the case, that it would be impossible for a jury, resolving all conflicts in favor of the Government and giving the evidence as to [the] San Francisco and Los Angeles episodes its utmost sweep, to find that advocacy of action was also engaged in when the group involved was thought particularly trustworthy, dedicated, and suited for violent tasks.

. . . [F]rom time to time instructions emanated from the Boards or their members to instructors of groups at lower levels. And while none of the written instructions produced at the trial were invidious in themselves, it might be inferred that additional instructions were given which were not reduced to writing. . . . As to these nine petitioners, then, we shall not order an acquittal.

Before leaving the evidence, we consider it advisable, in order to avoid possible misapprehension upon a new trial, to deal briefly with petitioners' contention that the evidence was insufficient to prove the overt act required for conviction of conspiracy. . . . Only 2 of the 11 overt acts alleged in the indictment to have occurred within the period of the statute of limitations were proved. Each was a public meeting held under Party auspices at which speeches were made by one or more of the petitioners extolling leaders of the Soviet Union and criticizing various aspects of the foreign policy of the United States. At one of the meetings an appeal for funds was made. . . . The Government concedes that nothing unlawful was shown to have been said or done at these meetings, but contends that these occurrences nonetheless sufficed as overt acts. . . . We think the Government's position is correct. It is not necessary that an overt act be the substantive crime charged in the indictment as the object of the conspiracy. . . . The function of the overt act in a conspiracy prosecution is simply to manifest "that the conspiracy is at work," . . . . The substantive offense here charged as the object of the conspiracy is speech rather than the specific action that typically constitutes the gravamen of a substantive criminal offense. . . . [W]e are not prepared to say that one of the episodes relied on here could not be found to be in furtherance of such an objective, if, under proper instructions, a jury should find that the Communist Party was a vehicle through which the alleged conspiracy was promoted. . . .

Justice Black (Justice Douglas concurring) registered a separate opinion, of which excerpts follow:*

I would reverse every one of these convictions and direct that all the defendants be acquitted. In my judgment the statutory provisions on which these prosecutions are based abridge freedom of speech, press and assembly in violation of the First Amendment of the U.S. Constitution. . . .

I believe that the First Amendment forbids Congress to punish people for talking about public affairs, whether or not such discussion incites to action, legal or illegal. . . . As the Virginia Assembly said in 1785, in its "Statute for Religious Liberty," written by Thomas Jefferson, "it is time enough for the rightful purposes of civil government, for its officers to interfere when principles break out into overt acts against peace and good order. . . ."

The Court's opinion summarizes the strongest evidence offered against these [nine] defendants. This summary reveals a pitiful inadequacy of proof to show beyond a reasonable doubt that the defendants were guilty of conspiring to incite persons to act to overthrow the Government. . . . It seems unjust to compel these nine defendants, who have just been through one four-month trial, to go through the ordeal of another trial on the basis of such flimsy evidence. . . . I cannot agree that "justice" requires this Court to send these cases back to put these defendants in jeopardy again in violation of the spirit, if not the letter of the Fifth Amendment's provision against double jeopardy. . . .

[In re the public meetings] the Court holds that attendance at these lawful and orderly meetings constitutes an "overt act" sufficient to meet the statutory requirements. I disagree.

* THESE TWO JUSTICES also dissented in *Dennis et al.*

The requirement of proof of an overt act in conspiracy cases is no mere formality, particularly in prosecutions like these which in many respects are akin to trials for treason. Article III, Para 3, of the Constitution provides that "No persons shall be convicted of Treason unless on the Testimony of two witnesses to the same overt Act, or on confession in open Court." One of the objects of this provision was to keep people from being convicted of disloyalty to government during periods of excitement when passions and prejudices ran high, merely because they expressed "unacceptable" views.... The same reasons that make proof of overt acts so important in treason cases apply here. The only overt act which is now charged against these defendants is that they went to a constitutionally protected public assembly where they took part in lawful discussion of public questions, and where neither they nor anyone else advocated or suggested the overthrow of the U.S. government. Many years ago this Court said that "The very idea of a government, republican in form, implies a right on the part of its citizens to meet peaceably for consultation in respect to public affairs and to petition for a redress of grievances." ... In my judgment defendants' attendance at these public meetings cannot be viewed as an overt act to effectuate the object of a conspiracy as charged.

... Unless there is complete freedom for expression of all ideas, whether we like them or not, concerning the way government should be run and who shall run it, I doubt if any views in the long run can be secured against the censor. The First Amendment provides the only kind of security system than can preserve a free government—one that leaves the way wide open for people to favor, discuss, advocate, or incite causes and doctrines however obnoxious and antagonistic such views may be to the rest of us.

E. Message to the Membership* *By Robert W. Kenny*

The National Lawyers Guild today faces questions directed not only at its own organization, but at all democratic institutions. Indeed, the questioning has gone beyond the stage of debate; the antagonists have resorted to attack. The conquests of Nazism are not only military; with the victory of arms has spread an impression of Nazi efficiency, and rumor of its revolutionary force. Even across the oceans, it tends to spread a confusion of thought, and fear. The danger, which we are hastily meeting with plans for military defense, lies as much in our attitude of mind as in the possibility of armed aggression.

At this time, obviously the chief insistence of the National Lawyers Guild should be that the defense of democracy be put in the hands of its proven friends.

The Lawyers Guild is pledged by its constitution:

To aid in making the United States and the State Constitutions, the law, and administrative and judicial agencies of government responsive to the will of the American people; to protect and foster our democratic institutions and civil rights and liberties of all the people, and to aid in the adoption of laws for the economic and social welfare of the people.

The passing years have underscored these objectives. The tragedies, which the histories of the past months have written, have rendered the functions of the National Lawyers Guild increasingly vital to the life of our country.

If there is one thing that is clear from these tragic months it is that democracy was permitted to fail in practice long before the destructive, anti-democratic forces prevailed. Into the gap between the written, the avowed theory of democracy and the daily undemocratic practices, the wedge of defeat found its way.

*NATIONAL LAWYERS GUILD QUARTERLY, Vol. 3, No. 2, July 1940.

It is the business of all people to close that gap, to make the theory, the spirit of democratic institutions coincide with the day-to-day business of government, economy, and social relationships. That business is primarily the lawyers' business. It is peculiarly the business of the National Lawyers Guild.

No group of men and women is better fitted by training or conviction to assure our people that the effort of achieving the democratic ideal has not been abandoned, that it is going forth day by day, that the values which have guided the course of life and government and institutions in our continent have not been discarded.

We must be the first to recognize that our practice of democracy is inadequate, because it is in that recognition that our consciousness of danger is born. From this recognition we must move toward constructive action for making our words and our professions of democracy actually do the work they should do. By making democracy a living, growing process, beyond the utterances of political theologians, we can enlist the forces of our people, our continent and our institutions, we can make our democracy strong against the threats of Fascism and Nazism.

History shows that lawyers have been in the front ranks of battles for social progress. Today we can, by being something more than hired assistants for private interests, continue to keep our posts where the work is at its thickest. Lawyers played a great part in the unfolding of the "New Deal." Much of the legislation and social attitude comprehended in that phrase is here to stay; but it will need defenders; it will need energetic forces for its extension and development. I think we should acknowledge to ourselves that only by insisting upon its growth and development can we effectively prevent its decay.

Concretely, with a view to more immediate problems, I suggest we go forward with formulating means toward:

1. *Including as an essential part of defense, a development of an integrated economy, agriculture, and foreign trade which will function democratically and for the maximum benefit of all of our people, without special privileges.*
2. *A comprehensive program for the greatest development of the civil rights and liberties of the people.*
3. *A sympathetic approach to the problems of our alien population.*
4. *Defense of effective New Deal legislation and an extension of its application in the fields of social security, old age and health assistance, housing and agriculture.*

5. *Steady application to study of the problems of lawyers themselves, their professional opportunities, and their relations to society.*

The foregoing is but tentative and general, but indicates some of the things I think the Lawyers Guild must do if it is not to fail in its obligation to itself and to our times. The time is not merely opportune, but critical. Either the liberals do this, and with dispatch, or the play will be taken by those reactionary forces already moving toward command.

The lawyer has been rightly called the soldier of civil life. Long ago, his reputation for courage and trustworthiness caused society to place its most important weapons in his hands.

Those weapons, it must be remembered, were fashioned by other lawyers through centuries of constitutional debate, legislation, and judicial exposition.

Today, as in other times of crisis, the lawyer is being told that his arms were all right for dress parade purposes, but too dangerous for practical use.

Thousand of American lawyers know that this is not so. They know that the concepts of due process, equal justice, and respect of human rights were forged in the world-shaking struggles of the past, and are the best defense in the inevitable crises of the future.

The National Lawyers Guild today is the rallying point for every American lawyer who intends to stick by the guns that society has entrusted to the legal profession.

BIBLIOGRAPHY

Belfrage, Cedric, *The American Inquisition: 1945–60*, Bobbs-Merrill, N.Y., 1973.

Bessie, Alvah, *Inquisition in Eden*, Macmillan, 1965.

Bosworth, Allan R., *America's Concentration Camps*, W. W. Norton, N.Y., 1967.

Gunther, John, *Inside U.S.A.* (First Edition), Harper & Row, N.Y., 1947.

Hill, Gladwin, *Dancing Bear*, World Publishing, N.Y., 1968.

Kahn, Gordon, *Hollywood on Trial*, Boni & Gaer, N.Y., 1948.

Katcher, Leo, *Earl Warren, a Political Biography*, McGraw-Hill, N.Y., 1967.

Levy, Leonard W., *Origins of the Fifth Amendment*, Oxford University Press, N.Y., 1968.

MacDougall, Curtis D., *Gideon's Army* (3 vols.), Marzani & Munsell, N.Y., 1965.

McWilliams, Carey, *The Education of Carey McWilliams*, Simon & Schuster, N.Y., 1979.

Phillips, Herbert L., *Big Wayward Girl*, Doubleday, N.Y.. 1968.

Trumbo, Dalton, *Time of the Toad: Study of Inquisition in America*, Harper & Row, N.Y., 1972.

Miscellaneous papers from the Bancroft Library, University of California, Berkeley, on Kenny's career as Attorney General; and from the Meiklejohn Civil Liberties Institute Library, in Berkeley, on the early years of the National Lawyers Guild.

Interviews by the author with Kenny and others as indicated in the text.

INDEX

A.B.A., *see* American Bar Ass'n
Academy Awards, 76, 78, 106, 107
A.C.L.U., 19, 122, 125, 159, 161
Adams, John Quincy, 178
Adams, Sherman, 18*n*
Adler, Larry, 77
A.F.L., 17, 124, 143
Alameda County (Calif.), 36, 41
A.L.P., 72*n*, 170
Alperowitz, Gar, xvii
Amendment, *see* Constitution, U.S.
American Bar Ass'n, 122–123, 124–
   127 *passim*, 133, 134, 138,
   141
American Civil Liberties Union, 19,
   122, 125, 159, 161
American Council on Race Rela-
   tions, 49, 51
American Federation of Labor, 17,
   124, 143
American Labor Party, 72*n*, 170
American Legion, 43, 47, 48
Americans for Democratic Action,
   65
*An Uncommon Man, or Henry
   Wallace and 60 Million
   Jobs,* 66*n*
Anderson, Glenn, 46, 147
A.P., 6
Appeals Court, *see* Appellate Court,
   U.S., or Appellate Court,
   Calif.
Appellate Court, Calif., 34–35, 107,
   124*n*, 147, 153
Appellate Court, U.S., 39, 96, 101*n*,
   149, 125*n*, 139, 149
Arens, Richard, xvii
Arnold, Thurman, 94, 124, 129,
   133
Associated Press, 6
Ass'n of Motion Picture Pro-
   ducers, 79, 80–81, 82
Attorney general (Calif.), 36, 37,
   38, 40, 152

Kenny as, 31, 37–40, 43, 46–51,
   53, 54, 131, 149
Warren as, 25, 40, 42, 43–46,
   166
Attorney general, U.S., 131, 138,
   139, 144
Augmented Fifth (Amendment),
   104

Baha'i (religion), 28, 29, 149
Baldwin, C. B. ("Beanie"), 59
Ball, Joseph, 128, 140, 141, 163
Bancroft, Hubert Howe, 19
Bank of China, 149
   of Santa Monica, 23
   of Tombstone, 21
   of Tuscon, 23
Bar Ass'n, American, 122–123,
   124–127 *passim*, 133, 134,
   138, 141
   L.A. County, xi, 140, 141
Bar, California State, 8, 34
Baseball, xiv, xv, xvi, 21, 22, 23,
   77–78, 159
Bemis, Luisa Moreno, 143
Benson, Elmer, 125
Berkeley (Calif.), 69; *see also*
   University of Calif. at
   Berkeley
Berle, Adolph, 124, 129–133
   passim
Bessie, Alvah, 78, 97, 112
Best Years of Our Lives, The, 76
Biberman, Herbert, 78, 91, 97,
   99*n*, 107, 112
Bill of Rights, 26, 79, 92, 166,
   176, 177
Birch (John) Society, xvii, 152,
   161
Black, Hugo, 97, 98, 119*n*, 133,
   175, 176, 181, 183
Blue Book, The, 47, 51
Bond, Carrie Jacobs, 19
Bone, Homer, 125